Praise for *Unmasking What Matters*

"Theater fans will love the insiders' stories culled from Sandra's years on Broadway—but absolutely anyone, regardless of their familiarity with theater, can and will benefit from the lessons contained in these pages. It's impossible to read this book and come out on the other side feeling anything but awakened."
  —**Jack Canfield,** Coauthor of the *Chicken Soup for the Soul®* series and *The Success Principles™: How to Get from Where You Are to Where You Want to Be*

"Sandra Joseph is a tender and clear soul whose journey unpacks what it means to hear your voice, and whose voice touches the center we all share."
  —**Mark Nepo,** author of *The Book of Awakening* and *The One Life We're Given*

"As a speaker, a writer, a singer, and a deep soul, Sandra Joseph shares her authentic voice to transform people's lives. Her message of *Unmasking What Matters* will give you the courage and conviction to play the leading role in your own life story. In this heartfelt book, she shares her own struggle to remove fear from center stage and instead put love front and center—and she provides you with the tools, and courage, you need to do the same."
  —**Marci Shimoff,** #1 *New York Times* best-selling author of *Happy for No Reason* and *Chicken Soup for the Woman's Soul*

"Have you ever wondered how some people get the courage to go after what they really want? They get it by identifying what's important and persevering in their pursuit of it DESPITE doubts and disappointments. Sandra Joseph pulls back the curtain and dares to reveal what really happens on the long road to success. You'll appreciate her honest insights, her put-you-in-the-scene storytelling and her inspiring wisdom about how she unmasked and honored what really matters - and how you can too."

—**Sam Horn,** author of *Got Your Attention* and *SOMEDAY is Not a Day in the Week*

"Drawing on her personal experiences on and off the stage, as well as cutting edge research, Sandra Joseph provides the information, tools, and loving support needed to move through blocks and take your life to the next level."

—**JJ Virgin,** *New York Times* best-selling author of *The Virgin Diet*

"What does it take to claim a new story and live the life we came to live? In *Unmasking What Matters*, Sandra Joseph shows us it is possible to release the roles we've been assigned to take center stage in our own lives. Whether she's sharing her message on the page or on the stage, she will take you by the heart and guide you home to your own center and your own voice. Here, you learn it is safe to love who you already are and lead your own life, unmasked."

—**Gail Larsen,** author and teacher, *Transformational Speaking: If You Want to Change the World, Tell a Better Story*

"Full of compassion and hard-won wisdom, *Unmasking What Matters* is a gentle, uplifting road-map back to the self. "

—**Barnet Bain,** director of *Milton's Secret*, producer of *What Dreams May Come*

Unmasking
What Matters

10 Life
Lessons
from
10 Years on
Broadway

Sandra Joseph

swp

SHE WRITES PRESS

Published 2018
Printed in the United States of America
ISBN: 978-1-63152-397-7 pbk
ISBN: 978-1-63152-398-4 ebk
Library of Congress Control Number: 2017958666

For information, address:
She Writes Press
1563 Solano Ave #546
Berkeley, CA 94707

She Writes Press is a division of SparkPoint Studio, LLC.

Interior design by Tabitha Lahr
Mask Logo © Debbie Prinz, Prinz Marketing Communications

Photos used with permission from Joan Marcus, The Really Useful Group, The Phantom Company

For my dad, whose care made everything possible.
For my mom, whose sensitivity is her strength.
For Monica, whose heart holds up the world
For Ron, whose superpower is love.

We never know when we will blossom into what we're supposed to be. It might be early. It might be late. It might be after thirty years of failing at a misguided way. Or the very first time we dare to shed our mental skin and touch the world.

—Mark Nepo

Contents

Introduction:

The Role of a Lifetime

It is clear that I have traveled through life thirsting for what was inside all along, while focused externally on the ever-changing horizon of achievement and opportunity. I have identified with my changing roles more than with the Inner Light, which is immortal. I have suffered from a case of mistaken identity.

—Joan Borysenko

The year after I left *Phantom*, two things happened that reshaped me: I was diagnosed with a tumor at the entry point of my brain, and my beloved father—my first and biggest fan—died suddenly. I found myself immersed in a felt sense of the unpredictability of life and a renewed awareness of limited time. The urgency I experienced surprised me. It had nothing to do with playing another role in a Broadway show. What I wanted more than anything was to be able to fully inhabit the role of Sandra Joseph, without embellishment or apology—something I had never quite known how to do.

From the start, I was a most unlikely Broadway star. A shy, highly sensitive kid who went out of her way to avoid being the center of attention, I didn't find the courage to step into the spotlight for years. But after decades of personal development, singing and acting training, and more rejection than I care to remember, I became the leading lady in Andrew Lloyd Webber's *The Phantom of the Opera*, Christine Daaé—a role in which I would make history.

The fact that I hold the record as Broadway's longest-running female star is still hard for me to wrap my head around. I played Christine some 1,300 times, performing six nights a week for nearly a decade. Many of those nights, as grateful as I was to have achieved my childhood dream of performing, my insecurity robbed me of feeling worthy of my position; I often went home after the show feeling like a failure and a fraud. The unhealed wounds of my past were just as present in the star dressing room as they had been on the playgrounds of my youth. As the years went by, I learned firsthand the truth in Jon Kabat-Zinn's wise words, "wherever you go, there you are."

I know I'm not alone. All too often, many of us make the mistake of thinking that some future accomplishment will somehow change the way we feel about ourselves. We tremble in the wings, paralyzed by self-doubt and fear. We feel stuck and small, lacking the self-confidence to move in the direction of what we really want. Or, if we do have the confidence, we work and struggle and achieve, exhausting ourselves with all of our emotion and activity—and yet somehow, no matter our level of outer-world success, we come up short. The happiness we were sure would accompany our success just isn't there, and we are left wondering what all that striving was for.

As social media creates a climate of "compare despair," it's becoming increasingly difficult to untether our minds from the belief that *there* will be better than *here*. Despite the abundance of current research proving that success for achievement's sake does not lead to happiness, more and more people are desperately seeking fame and fortune. One 2017 study found that more than a quarter of millennials would quit their job in exchange for fame, one in ten would choose fame over a college degree, and one in twelve would cut off their own family to be a household name. Our lightning-paced world keeps us all on a treadmill of doing, addicted to the climb, never getting to a place of "enough."

Don't get me wrong. I'm a fan of achievement (and millennials). It's gratifying to give it all you've got and reap the rewards. But after reaching the pinnacle of my profession, I can say one thing for sure: the journey up is no substitute for the journey in. Success that satisfies over the long term requires something more than external accolades, and that's because self-worth is an inside job. We're not good enough because of what we do. We're good enough because of who we are. We are worthy by virtue of the fact that we are here—each imperfect one of us—as a living, breathing, invaluable part of the unfathomable universe.

So, how can we bring what is inside us out into the world in a way that is in alignment with our deepest values? How can we choose the path of love over the path of fear—the path that leads to our greatest peace, potential, success, and fulfillment? If we were to live our lives full out, what would that look like? This book invites you to seek the wisdom of your own heart for the answers to these and many other essential questions.

In the ten chapters that follow, I share the story of how I moved through crippling self-doubt, shyness, and stage fright to become *Phantom*'s leading lady—and, even more important, the ten biggest lessons that journey taught me.

I'm excited to share with you the tools and practices that have made the biggest difference in my life, many of them curated from some of the leading psychologists, social scientists, and spiritual thinkers of our time.

I learned so much on the road to Broadway and in the decade I spent as Christine that has helped me inhabit the role of Sandra more fully. Listening to my inner voice, practicing self-compassion, and learning how to stand in my field of power is what got me a starring role on Broadway; the greater gift, though, has been that these same principles and practices have helped me to inhabit my truth and become more of my authentic self. The means, it turns out, were also ends in and of themselves. All those years I was trying to get *there*, only to discover that landing *here* was actually what I was seeking all along.

After you read this book, I hope you will be inspired to believe in bigger possibilities for yourself—that you will achieve every outrageous goal and improbable dream your mind can muster. But my heart's deepest wish for you, dear reader, is that you will cultivate the courage to stand in your authentic presence, build a life full of meaning, and love the real you—the you behind the mask.

Learning to love our unmasked selves is an epic journey. It begins with the courage to look. Let's go.

Chapter 1:

See Behind the Mask

To see through the veil that our senses and our thinking minds make real, to see behind the mask to true self, feels like the highest aspiration of humanity. Because, as we are able to do that, it's as if we are able to find our rightful place in the order of things. We recognize a harmony that's been waiting for us to feel.

—Ram Dass

"You try my patience! Make. Your. Choice." The seething Phantom hisses his ultimatum to my desperate Christine in the final scene of the show. Either she stays imprisoned with him forever in his underground lair or he will murder her fiancé, who stands nearby, his neck encircled in a noose.

What Christine does next was my favorite moment to play. There is no more raging, pleading, cowering, or flee-ing. Exhausted from the battle, she suddenly recognizes how deeply the man with the deformed face must have suffered to cause him to act out in this way. Her heart softens, as hearts often do when confronted with the pain and suffering of another, and in that tender moment, she becomes the embodiment of compassion: she takes hold of the Phantom's face—his unmasked face—looks directly at the source of his shame, and responds to that shame with love. Earlier in the play, when she first lifts the mask from the Phantom's face, she recoils and runs away in horror—but by this final, climactic scene, she is able to embrace what she once feared and love the totality of the flawed human being before her.

Phantom has become the most lucrative entertainment enterprise of all time not only because of its beautiful music and crashing chandelier, but also because the story connects to something very deep in the human psyche. We all know what it is to want to cover up some aspect of ourselves. Far too much suffering is caused by the belief that we are somehow flawed at our core. *If you really saw me*, we think, *you would find me unlovable, unworthy, unimportant, not good enough.*

I played the scene I just described more than a thousand times over the course of a decade, and yet somehow, in all those years, I failed to receive the powerful message it held. It was only after I left the show, after events beyond my control changed the way I saw the world, that I learned the lesson that had been staring me in the face for so long: the key to everything we are seeking lies in our willingness to live an unmasked life.

Remember Your Essence

Perhaps we're closest to an unmasked life when we're children, before the mind and its incessant chatter trap us, when we are simply immersed in the joyful experience of being alive. Young children, after all, have no use for masks, unless they're playing make-believe. When they are being themselves, they are utterly authentic and often closer to the wonder and joy of being alive than adults are.

One beautiful spring day when I was four, I sat on the sun-soaked porch of my family's Harvard Street duplex in Detroit, drawing a sun with a yellow Crayola, when the nice lady who lived upstairs came down to talk to me. We'd been chatting for a while when she posed a question I wasn't expecting: "Where did you come from?" she asked, tilting her head and catching my eye.

It was a funny question, but I immediately understood what she meant. She was not asking how I'd come to be sitting on the porch that afternoon. She was asking, "How did you come to be in the world?"

I looked at her, bemused, wondering how it was possible that she didn't know the answer. To me, it was as plain as the yellow on the paper in my lap. But I answered politely, with a quiet self-assurance: "I've always been here." I would have just as readily assured her that she, my dog, and the lilac tree in the yard had always been there and always would be. Maybe the forms would change, but the essence, the life within the life, had no beginning and no end. I didn't have the language to articulate it, but I remember the deep inner sense of connection I felt. Everything was eternal. It seemed so obvious. There was nowhere to go that was better than where I was.

We have all experienced those rare moments of pure being, when time seems to stop. In those eternal instants, we sense that there is a profound connection between all life and that somehow the oneness that we are touches the timeless. We are suddenly awake for a moment to the truth of things—we get a glimpse of the capital-"S" Self—and we wonder how we ever could have forgotten it.

But then the moment passes and the insight fades from memory because in our increasingly distracted world, it's not easy to remember who we truly are. With age comes a film-ing-over of the essential self, and before we know it, many of us find ourselves separated from our direct experience of life.

In the years that followed that exchange on my front porch, I would hear a call that would move me far away from my Michigan home and into the world. Incredible adventures were to follow, in which some dreams were dashed and others were fulfilled beyond my wildest imag-inings. All that time, I thought the dreams were what I was seeking. I thought they were the end goal. What I under-stand now is that the point of the pursuit was to get back to that total immersion, that timeless sense of connection and oneness, I experienced on that sunlit porch in Detroit when I was four.

Shed Mistaken Identities

In the 1910 Gaston Leroux novel in which the character of the Phantom (named Erik in the book) first appeared, he wears a mask that covers his entire, deformed face. At one point, Erik mentions that he first donned the mask because his own mother found his appearance too horrific to look at.

The masks we wear in our daily lives may be a lot more subtle than Erik's, but our impulse to put them on often originates from a similar place: a feeling that something within us is unacceptable and must be hidden from view.

Psychologist Gail Brenner has one answer for where we get the masks—or limiting identities—we wear: other people. More specifically, she says, those who look at us through the lens of their own biases, judgments, and projections—Erik's mother, for example—nudge us into obscuring our true selves. And according to Dr. Brenner, it's up to us to reject and shed what she calls "these mistaken identities."

Shelly Lefkoe, cofounder of the Lefkoe Institute, iden-tifies another place masks can come from: our own beliefs.

"Unfortunately," she says, "most of us adopt negative beliefs about ourselves from experiences, even those with our (often well-meaning) primary caregivers, including our parents." And after decades of working with people's harmful beliefs, Lefkoe reports, there are several she's heard again and again. These are the most common:

- I'm not good enough.
- What makes me good enough is having other people think well of me.
- Mistakes and failure are bad.
- What makes me good enough is achievement.
- I'm worthless.

Any of those sound familiar? They are just the sorts of thoughts our inner judge, a subtle but powerful mask-maker, has been whispering to many of us for years. All kinds of masks—masks of nonchalance and arrogance, of anger and feigned pleasure, of superiority and inferiority—are created and worn because we think they protect us. At some point, they probably did. Many of us learned to behave in a certain way to avoid harm when we were kids. We learned to edit ourselves, to play small, and to keep parts of ourselves under wraps in order to be accepted or stay safe. But what was once a survival strategy has become a way of showing up that is limited—not the truest version of ourselves, not the fullest expression of who we know ourselves to be on the inside.

Just before I entered fifth grade, my family moved from the bottom half of a six-hundred-square-foot, two-bedroom duplex in Detroit to a modest three-bedroom house in the suburb of Harper Woods. We were on the very farthest edge of the Grosse Pointe school district, the part locals referred to as "the ghetto of Grosse Pointe," and I was suddenly thrust into classrooms filled with wealthy kids who had spent the weekend playing tennis or boating at the yacht club. Instantly, everything about me was not right. I wore the wrong clothes and shoes. My family could not afford the designer labels my friends wore. I didn't have the right kind of bike and, later, car.[1] I felt, as many of us do, that I had to be somehow different in order to belong.

Then, and for many years after, feeling that I was "less than" put me—as it puts many of us—in a cycle of trying to self-improve or achieve my way into feeling good enough. I spent too much energy in the fruitless pursuit of trying to prove my worth. I spent too much time wearing the mask of Who I Think I Should Be, failing to realize that I, like everyone, actually had nothing to prove or improve in order to be good enough. Many of us feel, as I did for much of my life, that we have to be other than we are in order to measure up. And while we understand, at least on some level, that the worthiness we seek can never be found in anything external or conditioned, we spend lifetimes of energy trying to prove our worth and earn our right to be here.

Embrace Your Inherent Worth

I once read a diet book that began in a most unexpected way. Instead of talking about what to eat or not to eat, the author started by discussing how to make your brain happy, explaining that if you didn't start with this (by balancing hormones, getting the chemistry right, et cetera), you would have very little hope of being successful with any of the nitty-gritty food recommendations that were forthcoming in the book.

I feel similarly about what I'm about to share with you in the nine chapters that follow this one. Without starting from a baseline of fundamental belief in your own worthiness, you

---

1. I'll never forget how excited I was to inherit my grandpa's old brown Caprice until my friend pulled up my driveway in his shiny, new red Ferrari (a gift for his sixteenth birthday). Yes, I'm talking that type of wealth.

have little hope of being successful at any of the rest of what you'll find in this book. I am going to give you the best of what I've learned—and am still learning—in the hope that it will help you raise your life to the grandest vision you hold for yourself. But if we don't begin by laying a foundation of authentic self-worth, none of it will matter. If there's a sense of inadequacy sitting in the driver's seat of your life, you won't get anywhere that makes any real difference.

We must begin with the biggest and most important lesson of this book: you—unmasked you—are enough, truly. Through and through, thoroughly and completely, absolutely, profoundly enough. It's easy to get so caught up in the comedy and tragedy of our lives, so identified with our subpersonalities, our issues, our stories, that we forget the larger whole of who we are. We forget that there is a fundamental nobility in the mere fact of being. Life has been gifted to us. We've each been cast in the role of being a particular, singular human within a set of given circumstances. None of us auditioned for the part we received, but we are exactly right for it, and now it's up to us to play that role full out.

I am using this rather heavy-handed theatrical metaphor not to be cute but to help point to an important truth: that the essence of who we are is perfect. A person is not a self-help project. We are not human *doings* who need to constantly strive to improve or achieve our way to okayness. Being you is your birthright. There is no need to put on a persona of any kind in order to be good enough.

So let's begin by taking a kind, compassionate, gentle look at who you are behind the mask. What would happen if you were brave enough to take an honest look at yourself? Not to put on rose-colored glasses and see only your proudest moments, but to really have the courage to remove the mask from your own face, examine with clear eyes and a kind heart the things you find unacceptable about yourself, and choose, once and for all, to love and respect the flawed human being that is there? Christine does not overlook the worst of the Phantom. She sees the totality of who he is— and she loves him completely anyway. What if we could have the courage to really see all of ourselves and love and respect ourselves anyway? What might happen?

Once you are grounded in authentic self-worth, you just might find yourself wanting to express something. To create something. To shine in the role you and only you were born to play. To make your life into a work of art that is a true reflection of who you are in all of your unmasked, imperfect glory. And you might be surprised to discover that your greatest fulfillment comes not from climbing to the top but from landing wholeheartedly where you are. Because as we give our all in pursuit of what we think we want, sometimes we wind up getting what we actually long for: the inner peace of being at home in our own skin, expressing our inner self in the outer world, and blossoming into all we were born to be.

It's not helpful to be told we are enough, of course, if deep down we just don't buy it. So, how can we change our relationship with ourselves and befriend the being that's wearing our name tag? One thing is clear: we must begin to shift our thoughts and beliefs. There are a number of practices, tools, and exercises that can help us unlearn negative beliefs, become less judgmental of ourselves, and develop our capacity to trust that it's safe to live out in the open, unmasked, and love the totality of who we are. Mirroring love is one of them.

Mirroring Love

A practice of harnessing the power of your own loving heart and turning that love toward yourself

1. Imagine someone you love fiercely. Gather your lion/lioness energy. Whom would you protect with all your might?

2. Imagine that someone harmed that person and they came to you feeling wounded. How would you respond? Think about the power of your love—the force field you can create with your own loving heart. Let yourself feel it.

3. Turn your fierce, loving heart toward itself like a mirror is being held up in front of you and reflecting all of that love back to you. Turn the power of your loving heart toward itself. Speak to yourself the way you would speak to a hurting child. Touch your hand the way you would touch the hand of someone you care about when they are suffering. Hold your own hand—literally—the way you would hold the hand of someone you love when they are gripped by fear or sadness, in that gesture that says, *I'm here for you. I've got you. We'll get through this together. I love you.*

4. Sit with the power of this love. Feel its healing energy.

   As the Buddha said, "You could search the whole world and never find anyone as deserving of love as yourself."

Take In the Good

Even after a thousand performances, the climactic scene in which Christine embraces the unmasked Phantom moved me.

I loved playing that scene; I can still remember the feeling. Imagine what it feels like to stand as the embodiment of loving acceptance. Imagine what it's like to hold that space for another. Imagine getting to be a conduit of unconditional loving presence. Even though I was playing a character, I, Sandra, could feel it was a sacred moment. And yet many nights, after changing out of my wig and costume, instead of being able to hold myself in that same loving acceptance, I judged myself. I picked apart my performance, focusing on the one note I hadn't hit the way I'd wanted to or the one moment when I hadn't been as present as I knew I should have been.

It's so easy, after all, to see only our flaws. When I first read about the evolutionary "negativity bias" in the human brain, I actually found it quite reassuring. Turns out it's not our fault that we find fault! Our brains are actually programmed to focus more on the negative than on the positive, as neuroscience researchers have demonstrated. In one study by John Cacioppo, participants were hooked up to equipment that recorded electrical activity in their brain and then were shown three types of pictures: images known to elicit positive feelings (e.g., a pizza); images designed to elicit negative feelings (e.g., a mutilated face); and images designed to elicit neutral feelings (e.g., a hair dryer). What Cacioppo found was remarkable. There was a significantly greater surge in electrical activity in the brains of his subjects when they were shown the negative images. In other words, we react much more strongly to—are much more heavily influenced by—the negative than we are by the positive.

Overall, this natural attribute is a good thing. If we weren't so aware of the dangers around us, humankind wouldn't have survived. But it isn't helpful that our moods, beliefs, and expectations—even those about ourselves—consequently skew negative. According to Dr. Rick Hanson, PhD, psychologist and author of *Hardwiring Happiness*, we are like Velcro for the negative and like Teflon for the positive.

It takes effort to balance the scales toward the positive to counteract the negativity bias in the brain. This is why Dr. Hanson advocates a practice he calls "taking in the good."

Absorbing what is good is a skill we would be wise to practice regularly. With practice, Rick says, we can actually level our cerebral playing field. We can't help but stay attuned to the negative, but taking in the good ensures we capture and savor positive experiences, too.

He suggests three steps:

1. Look for good facts, and turn them into good experiences.
2. Sustain your enjoyment of the experience.
3. Let yourself absorb the experience.

If you're not sure how to put that third step into practice, check out what Rick Hanson writes about how people allow goodness to seep into their being:

People do this in different ways. Some feel it in their body like a warm glow spreading through their chest like the warmth of a cup of hot cocoa on a cold wintry day. Others visualize things like a golden syrup sinking down inside, bringing good feelings and soothing old places of hurt, filling in old holes of loss or yearning; a child might imagine a jewel going into a treasure chest in her heart. And some might simply know conceptually, that while this good experience is held in awareness, its neurons are firing busily away, and gradually wiring together.

Even before I read Rick Hanson's work, I was already doing my own version of taking in the good: during my time in *Phantom*, to counteract my tendency to beat up on myself for what hadn't gone perfectly in my performance, I began challenging myself to write down five things that I'd done well every night after a show. My list often included simply having the courage to show up in front of some 1,500 people. (As you'll learn in Chapter 2, I was not immune to the fear of public speaking—or acting, or singing—that most people experience.) Rick Hanson's guidelines for taking in the good about ourselves and our lives, however, have taken my practice to an entirely new level and significantly changed my life for the better.

It's helpful to make taking in the good a habit, because, as the popular phrase goes, "Neurons that fire together, wire together." Focusing on the positive once or twice may have only a tiny impact, but if we continue the practice over time, it can make a marked difference in our brain and throughout our being.

Change Your Vocabulary

There's a story about the Dalai Lama that has become rather famous. He was speaking to a large gathering of renowned teachers and psychologists when one of them asked how to help Western meditation students overcome self-hatred. His Holiness is fluent in English, but he turned to his translator with a confused look on his face when the question was put forth. He didn't understand what was being asked, because there is no word in Tibetan for "self-hatred."

They went back and forth for some time before the wise teacher finally understood. When the translator finally communicated the concept in a way he could grasp, His Holiness's response was emphatic: "But this is a mistake!" he cried.

It surely is.

The number one lesson of my ten years on Broadway is the importance of seeing myself, and others, the way Christine sees the Phantom in that climactic scene. We can actively practice looking at the world through eyes of unconditional love and acceptance, and we can make a habit of staying present to the truth behind the mask—the oneness of all things. This begins with remembering who we are underneath all roles, personas, projections, and expectations others have put on us or we have put on ourselves. Getting back in touch with our original goodness gives us courage to go where we are destined to go and align our outer lives with our inner truth.

It is impossible to overstate how much I have been impacted by the work of poet, teacher, author, and philosopher Mark Nepo. It was from Mark that I first learned that the origin of the word "honor" means "to keep in view what is true" and that the word "respect" means "to look again"—"re-spect." We respect and honor ourselves and one another by taking another look and seeing not the surface but the soul. To honor (to keep in view what is true) each other means seeing behind the mask of everyone we meet. It means recognizing that we are each other, and seeing that everything is connected to everything else.

Of course, being human, it isn't possible to be this aware every minute of every day. But we can look for moments of true seeing, and when we find them, we can savor them. When we do keep what is true in view, we recognize that behind each earth suit is a walking miracle—one that is made of the very same star-stuff we are.

Show Your True Face

Full recognition of who we are is the doorway to everything we seek; it begins by reclaiming our authentic essence, returning to our true self. For some of us, it's been a long time since we've had moments of openhearted, directly felt experience of aliveness. But that's where the treasure is buried. It's already within each one of us, just waiting to be discovered and brought to the surface, where it can become part of the way we forge meaning out of the life we've been gifted.

So let me say this before we go any further: You are not what you've done or haven't done. Your achievements or failures don't define you. You are good enough because you were born that way. You are worthy because you are here. You are a living miracle—connected to the living universe. On some level, you already know this. The challenge for all of us is to embrace this knowledge and to allow it to guide us in our daily lives. This is the journey we'll take together in the nine chapters ahead.

As we begin, I invite you to take a vow of absolute kindness toward your own being, to see what Thomas Merton called "the secret beauty" of your heart. "If only they could see themselves as they really are," Merton wrote. "If only we could see each other that way all the time, there would be no more war, no more hatred, no more cruelty, no more greed. . . . I suppose the big problem would be that we would fall down and worship each other."

I ask that you remember your most pure and innocent self—the you that you may remember feeling into as a small child, the you that is infinite, spacious, and free. I invite you to feel into your original essence, to respect yourself so thoroughly that honoring who you are becomes the foundation from which you live and breathe and move.

Questions to Live By*

- Who are you beyond the roles you play?

- Who are you beyond your body, your history, your possessions, and even your beliefs, thoughts, opinions?

- Who would you be if there were no problems to solve?

- Do you feel you have to earn your worth or change something about yourself in order to be okay?

- Can you find the courage to shed your limiting identities?

* Download the *Unmasking What Matters* journal and other freely offered resources at **www.sandrajoseph.com/bookgifts**.

Chapter 2:

Obey Your Instincts

*Let yourself be silently drawn by the strange
pull of what you really love. It will not lead you
astray.*

—Rumi

By the time I was five or six, the only evidence of my father's
acting career that remained was the box of 8x10 black-
and-white glossies—photos of a younger, thinner version of
the man I knew—that he kept in the basement. But when my
dad was a young man, he acted in community theater produc-
tions in Detroit. He played Biff in *Death of a Salesman* and
Tom in *The Glass Menagerie*—and if he hadn't had to drop
out of the play before opening night because my mother was
having pregnancy complications, he would have played Oscar
in *The Little Foxes,* too. That was the end of his stage career;
after I was born, he never acted again. There was simply no
time with two little girls on the scene.

From early on, though, he taught my sister and me that singers and actors were magic. He lit up every time he heard Sinatra; his jaw dropped when he watched Brando or Newman onscreen. His respect for the craft of acting—especially for "all those Method guys"—bordered on worship. Still, I never scented even a whiff of resentment or disappointment on him—no bitterness over the fact that he had had to give up the limelight to take care of his family. He was perfectly content to be a fan and share his love of theater with the three leading ladies in his life.

When I was little, my dad and I spent a lot of time in our basement, sitting atop my grandmother's old floral sofa, listening to records. In those days, I insisted the Bee Gees were the finest singers in the world, but my dad relentlessly force-fed me Sinatra, Nat King Cole, and Mel Tormé. "Listen to how he hits this note," Dad would say, holding his index finger in the air in breathless anticipation of one of the crooner's soaring baritones. Blissful hours passed down there, both of us drunk with music, with singers singing. As I got older, Dad would sit in his recliner upstairs and I'd be across from him on the plaid sofa, watching him rewind the VCR to repeatedly take in the brilliant moments from his favorite films. "Just watch this real quick—when Sonny leaves the room, watch what he does. He's so brilliant." My dad had seen *The Godfather* hundreds of times, but Brando's genius made him so giddy that he always busted out laughing with every viewing, slapping the arm of his recliner and rewinding it a half dozen times before he was done. The sheer joy that emanated from him in those moments could shake the weight off of even my darkest teenage moods.

But there was a high that went beyond the thrill of great acting and singing, and that was when the two art forms came together: when singers acted; when actors sang. My first taste of the magic of musicals was in the movies. By the time I reached adolescence, I had repeatedly devoured *The*

Wizard of Oz, The Sound of Music, Mary Poppins, and *West Side Story.* Musicals were so real to me as a kid that I half expected groups of people in the streets to break into four-part harmony and high kicks when I left the house.

I heard there was an entire city full of musicals. I pictured Broadway as some far-off fairy-tale land where theaters lined the streets and were as close together as the houses in our neighborhood, where real, live, singing actors performed elaborate shows with singing and dancing and costumes and sets night after night. I became obsessed with a story about a young orphan whose dog had my name. I listened to the soundtrack over and over again and sang the songs in an endless loop when I was alone in the basement.

Then, one Christmas morning when I was eight or nine, I received a gift that would change my life forever. After my sister, Monica, and I had torn through yards of wrapping paper, we collapsed into our brand-new beanbag chairs to survey the loot: the latest Donny & Marie album for Monica, a Shaun Cassidy T-shirt for me, Shrinky Dinks and a Lite-Brite for us both. Our ignorance of how tight money was tended to hit its blissful peak at Christmastime. My parents always managed to somehow make the holidays feel abundant, and that year had been no exception.

I lounged on my beanbag chair for only a few minutes before I realized a crucial element of the morning was missing: I had almost forgotten about my stocking! I raced over to the fake fireplace to see what fruit would be bulging out this year, Monica close on my heels. When we reached them, we stopped cold; the stockings were flat. I stood in front of mine and stared, willing it to somehow fill itself.

My parents watched the scene with amusement. "Look inside," my dad said, smiling.

I lifted the stocking off its hook and peered inside. Nestled at the bottom was an unmarked envelope. I was sure it was some boring McDonald's gift certificate. *Act excited*, I told myself, gearing up for disappointment, but what I found when I peeled the envelope open required no false display of enthusiasm. Inside was a red admission ticket that said one word in big black letters: *Annie*.

The night of the show, we filed into the Fisher Theatre amid the throngs of decked-out patrons. I felt glamorous and sophisticated. We took our seats (in the orchestra section!), and as the lights dimmed, my father took my hand in his.

The second the redheaded little girl playing Annie walked onstage, I was bitten—hard. Here was a girl my size and my age, up there singing and acting and dancing with total confidence and seemingly no fear. My longing to do what she was doing was so intense, it felt like physical pain. I spent the entire night out of my own skin, imagining myself in hers.

I will confess something to you now that I haven't been very open about in the past, even among my closest friends. At best, you may think me woo-woo, at worst, a self-aggrandizing magical thinker. But the truth is, I believe something deep within me actually did "see" myself up there onstage. Call it intuition, call it precognition, call it a childlike penchant for outside-the-box thinking—I just know that even before I had any inkling of whether or not I had anything resembling talent, there was some deep inner pocket of belief in my heart that I could and would perform onstage one day.

To me, a timid, introverted girl whose worst nightmare was having all eyes on her, that belief was utterly terrifying. On the surface, becoming a performer seemed impossible for someone like me. But in the depths of someplace I cannot name or explain, I also felt a kind of inevitability, an intuitive sense that this was to be my path—though I knew it would not be an easy one.

Maybe you've had a similar experience, where you knew something so deeply that you felt it in your whole body? And perhaps right on the heels of that knowing came a sense of doubt or disbelief?

It would take decades before I understood how entirely possible it is to feel conflicting emotions at the same time. That night, all I knew was that I was filled simultaneously with a sense of excitement and anticipation and a sense of loss over what I could never be.

When I climbed into the backseat for the drive home, I didn't say a word. I felt transparent, as if everyone could see straight into my aching heart, and I was afraid of what they would say. Every girl in that audience probably imagined being the one up there onstage. What would people say if I confessed to wanting to sing and act? Who was I to think I was so special? How could I ever explain that while I yearned to do it, the very thought also made me quake with fear?

I was the shy kid who hid behind my mother's thigh and trembled anytime a stranger looked at me sideways. Stand on a stage in front of a crowd by myself? Sing by myself in front of that crowd? Me? Not possible. It. Made. No. Sense. But love often grabs us by the heart in unexpected ways. Sometimes we are helpless to stop it. The wonderful news is this: when it comes to love, we find inner resources we didn't know we had.

Trust Your Heart

I've come to understand that we can actually trust the yearnings we feel in our chest and doing so isn't woo-woo at all. Compelling evidence suggests that the physical heart is capable of reaching beyond what most of us perceive to be normal limits of time and space. We tend to think of the brain as command central, but research in the field of neurocardiology (the brain in the heart!) has shown that the brain in the head isn't the only seat of intelligence in the human body. Turns out, intelligence isn't entirely a "top-down" equation. The heart actually communicates in an upward direction as well, sending important information to the brain.

In one study conducted by the HeartMath Institute, participants were shown pictures on a computer screen that were designed to be either emotionally arousing (a gun, a snake) or calming (a baby, a puppy). The researchers measured brain response (EEG) and heart-rhythm activity (ECG). What they found was incredible: not only did both the brain and the heart receive prestimulus information some four to five seconds *before* the computer randomly selected the images, but *the heart received the information a good 1.5 seconds before the brain did.*

According to HeartMath's extensive research, the heart, both physically and metaphorically, is the key to tapping into an intelligence that can powerfully improve our lives.

The heart communicates in four primary ways:

1. It sends neurological information to the brain and the rest of the body.
2. It sends energy through the body in the form of a blood pressure wave, which affects the electrical activity of brain cells.
3. It releases atrial peptide—a hormone that inhibits the release of other stress hormones—into the body.
4. It communicates electromagnetically. (This is what an electrocardiogram (EKG) measures: the electrical activity of your heart.)

Heart Inquiry
A practice of excavating important truths from the wisest place within you

HeartMath has developed a number of tools and techniques for tapping into the heart's intelligence. I've used their technologies for many years and have found them to be game-changers. Here's my variation on one of my favorite HeartMath tools:

1. Sit quietly and close your eyes.

2. Place both hands over your heart and breathe a little more deeply than you normally do—five to six seconds on each inhalation and exhalation. Imagine your breath is traveling into and out of your heart.

3. Imagine your mind slowly traveling down and curling up like a cat in your chest.

4. Ask your heart for guidance.

5. When you feel ready, open your eyes and get out your journal. Write for ten minutes, beginning with the following prompts:
    - "When I really listen inwardly, what I hear is . . ."
    - "If I'm really honest, what I yearn for is . . ."
    - "In a quiet corner of my heart, I know that . . ."

Obey Your Instincts

I'd been playing Christine on tour for about two years when the show got a new leading man: Ron Bohmer.[2] Before Ron took over the role of the Phantom on the national tour (the Raoul Company) in 1997, the two of us were flown to New York to rehearse with director Hal Prince.

We got to a scene called "The Final Lair," where the Phantom flies into a rage, and on the first run Ron did the blocking (onstage movement) exactly as he'd learned it. When we finished the scene, Hal asked us to try again. "I've believed everything you've done so far, but you just stopped telling the truth," he told Ron.

Ron and I exited the stage and entered the scene again—and this time, his performance took on a dynamism I had never experienced before. He veered slightly from the blocking. I followed his lead and unshackled myself from the way I was used to playing the scene. Ron, an intuitive and intelligent actor, moved swiftly away from me, then back toward me, pacing madly. The scene came alive.

"Yes! Better!" Hal shouted.

Ron hunched over, hands on his knees, face flushed and sweaty, and said to Hal, "Okay, good."

"Now start again, but go back to the blocking," Hal said.

"Sure," Ron nodded. "I was just obeying an instinct."

This is something actors are encouraged to do in training: to obey our instincts, follow our gut, and stay present in our bodies so we're open to all possibilities. We're taught not to edit ourselves. If we feel inclined to move, we move.

Would that we were all taught how to do the same in life.

We live in a culture that values facts over feelings. According to Francis P. Cholle, author of *The Intuitive Compass: Why the Best Decisions Balance Reason and Instinct*, in order to make good decisions, we need more than just rational thinking—we need intuition. But because our society is

---

2. *Five years after meeting in the show, Ron Bohmer and I took on new roles offstage: husband and wife.*

not particularly supportive of the idea of simply going with our gut, we often fail to utilize this important tool. "We are embarrassed to say that we follow hunches, we mistrust the sometimes-cryptic messages that our instincts send to us, and consequently we diminish our capacity to leverage the power of our own instincts when we need them most," says Cholle.

Our inner voice speaks to us throughout our lives. You know it when you hear it. Often, it says the most unlikely things.

Some people really listen when their inner voice speaks. Many entrepreneurs, for example, say that they make their decisions based primarily upon gut instinct—either they feel good about something or they don't, and they trust that feeling. Research supports this approach; in fact, a study conducted by business psychologist and author Chantal Burns indicates that professionals who follow their gut feelings will be right 70 percent of the time. Burns's study further found that overthinking a decision can have damaging effects on a business.

Apple founder Steve Jobs is perhaps the single most extraordinary example from the business world of someone who always listened to his inner wisdom and found great success in doing so. "Don't let the noise of others' opinions drown out your own inner voice," Jobs once said. "And, most important, have the courage to follow your heart and intuition." And it appears he followed his own advice. Take the iPad, one of the more risky products he took a chance on over the course of his career. When Jobs developed and launched that particular piece of technology, the industry barraged him with criticism: people said there was no market for it, that no one had any use for something that was neither a laptop nor a PDA. We all know what happened: The iPad became a breakout success, exceeding everyone's expectations.

My friend Susan was in her late thirties, divorced, and not finding her match on any of the dating sites she'd joined.

She wanted to change careers but feared giving up her steady paycheck. However, she also had a strong yearning she could not shake: she ached to become a mother. Susan found herself researching sperm banks, despite her rational mind telling her, *This. Makes. No. Sense.* Friends and family told her how difficult it would be to raise a child on her own, especially given her desire to leave her job and embark on an entirely new career path. They were full of questions: Shouldn't she figure out the job thing first? Would she have enough money to support both herself and a baby? She could not answer any of their logical questions. Still, she knew she would regret it if she didn't heed the call of her inner voice.

Her first attempt at pregnancy failed. Her second was ectopic. The journey was difficult, stressful, tearful. But if you asked her today whether she would do things differently, she would return a resounding no. Her son, Jack, is now a robust four-year-old. She did change careers. And today she is living with a partner and is stepmom to his two young children. None of it has been easy, but she says she is grateful every day that she let her inner wisdom guide her actions.

Focus On Your Heart's Desire
A practice of tuning in to your desires—and realizing them*

Sandra Selby's *The Five Minute Positive Focus Daily Journal* is a self-reflection journal that asks readers to take five minutes out of each day to answer the same set of questions. I've used this book for several years, and I've found that it's a wonderful morning ritual—a pleasurable, quick, and easy way to hear your inner voice and connect with your inner wisdom. Selby presents five questions in her journal, but here we'll focus on just two: "Divine Desires and Dreams" and "Positive Intention for Today."

1. Divine Desires and Dreams—What Is My "Heart's Desire"?
This question is about your dreams and desires of *all* sizes. We all have *big* dreams, as well as everyday, smaller desires. Put it all down, and repeat them as often as you would like . . . or do a new one every day. You can put down exactly what you would like to happen, or what you would like something to look like when it is complete. This will take the emotionality out of it, and the fears. Imagine that this is a perfect world and that you can have whatever you want. What would that be?

Example: "I see myself getting the job of my dreams— one that is both fulfilling and challenging."

2. Positive Intention for Today—A Step Toward My Dreams
This is your action step. You are putting your energy where your dreams are . . . and the universe will meet you tenfold. Make this step easy to handle, and you may end up adding other steps to it. Do not let yourself get overwhelmed with huge, unrealistic assignments that will stop the positive process before it has begun.

Example: "I will apply to one new job today that seems like a good fit for me."

Try devoting five minutes a day to this practice. You'll be amazed at how much easier it will make it for you to hear your inner voice when it has something to say!

*Adapted with permission from Sandra Selby

Embrace the Big

Our heart is speaking to us all the time, leading us to our fullest expression. Sometimes we hear its call like a siren from an early age. Sometimes we hear it when we're older, in barely a whisper. In either case, what calls to us often comes laced with fear and self-doubt, which can prevent us from trusting what we've heard. I invite you to trust your inner guidance, even—and perhaps especially—if what you hear seems too big for you.

Throughout our lives, we can practice turning inward to hear the voice of our own heart, the communication from our essential self. It is giving us invaluable information. The quiet inner yearning of the heart is a compass that points us in the direction of our aliveness and joy. When we take time to go within and bring our full attention to what lies in our depths, we find that we always know the right next step to take. We know that under the turbulent waves at the top of the ocean, there is stillness in the deep. When we still our minds and let the surface of our lives settle, the answers we seek rise up.

So get still, listen deeply, break the rules, make the unpopular move, trust your inner voice, do something different, create something new, try the thing you would never have tried five years ago. What have you got to lose? Probably a lot. But what have you got to gain? Everything that will make your life into a work of art that you and only you can create.

Questions to Live By

- What is the yearning in your heart?

- What is your "I could never" belief?

- Do you regularly carve out time to journey inward and actively listen to your inner voice? What might happen if you did?

Chapter 3:

Say Yes to Your Solo

*In any given moment we have two choices: to
step forward into growth or back into safety.*

—Abraham Maslow

"Five minutes. This is your five-minute call. Five minutes to
the top of Act One." The stage manager's voice echoed
through the small speaker in my dressing room. I was alone
and unhurried, putting the finishing touches on my Hanni-
bal outfit, snapping bejeweled bracelets around each wrist.
Erna, my dresser, had just headed back downstairs to the
wardrobe room after helping me into my corset and costume.
Leone, *Phantom*'s wig master, had exited after catching me
up on his cats and the latest repairs to his house in Yonkers
while carefully wrapping my hair under a stocking cap and
bobby-pinning the Christine wig to my head.

I stood in front of the full-length mirror, rubbing my
palms up and down the green and red velvet panels covering

my torso and combing my fingers through the gold tassels that hung from my hips to the tops of my pink ballet slippers. It was almost time to descend the flight of stairs to my left that led to the stage. But there was another flight of stairs to my right that beckoned to me many nights at this time: the fire escape stairs just outside my dressing room window. I stood in the center of the small, rectangular room, looking left, then right, then left again.

The rack of costumes I'd be wearing that night lined the entire wall between the two sets of stairs. Each gown had been built to my exact measurements and carried a price tag similar to that of a sports car. Some 1,500 people had taken their seats in the Majestic Theatre. Every single seat was filled every single night, even though the price of a ticket had crept to upwards of $125. The pressure of having to "bring it" was sometimes too much to bear. When the old voices of criticism started raging in my head, my feelings of unworthiness made those fire escape stairs seem so darn appealing. *What if I don't nail the high notes?* my inner voice demanded. *What if I'm not emotionally connected during the mausoleum scene? What if everyone in that audience can see that I'm not a real actress and singer but rather a scared kid from Detroit masquerading as a Broadway performer?*

The fire escape was right there. How easy it would be to climb down those stairs and disappear into the crowd of tourists in Times Square. I could move to Europe, change my name, grow a beard.

In my mind, I was back in fifth grade, two years after I saw *Annie*. I had just gotten my first big break: there was only one solo in the fifth-grade Christmas concert, and Mrs. Maters had given it to me. It wasn't a whole song, just a few lines, but I was over the moon. When the choir sang "The Christmas Song" ("Chestnuts roasting on an open fire . . ."), I was to sing along with the group until the song's bridge, and then I would get to step out from my spot, proceed to the microphone at the center of the stage, and have my diva moment, singing about Santa and his sleigh and all the presents he was bringing our way.

The solo would last only about ten seconds. Then I would walk back to my spot and sing the rest of the song with the choir. I hoped my handful of lines would be enough to inspire a talent scout to frantically run over to my parents and ask where in the world I'd been hiding because he needed to take me to New York and get me on Broadway immediately.

When the big day finally arrived, all of the fifth-graders, decked out in our holiday finery, lined up single file against the wall outside the gym. Mrs. Maters, our music teacher, was at the front of the line, peeking inside every couple of minutes to see whether it was time yet for us to make our big entrance. She held her hand high in the air, fingers spread wide. This was our five-minute warning. As one of the shorter kids in the class, I was almost at the back of the line. I would stand on the very bottom riser for the entire Christmas concert, visible from head to toe to the entire audience. I looked down the length of my scrawny body. Had I worn the right shoes? Was my dress too dressy? Worst of all, would I be able to choke out my solo? My cheeks were hot, my knees like Jell-O. I swallowed hard.

Mrs. Maters's strawberry-blond head turned to peek once more into the gym. I noticed one of the rear gym doors beside me. *Just one quick peek.* I pried the heavy green door open and saw a sea of colors, folding chairs, noise, parents, siblings—judgment, horror, humiliation. There were so many people out there. Who knew our tiny elementary school gymnasium could pack 'em in like that? So many bodies, so much noise. And there, in front of it all, that skinny little microphone stand, all by itself out in the naked, lonesome center of the stage.

My mouth went dry. Vomit rose in the back of my throat. The kids at the front of the line disappeared one by one into the gym. Mrs. Maters held the door open. There was no way I could stand up there and sing by myself in front of all those people! I had to find a way out—pronto! I raced to Mrs. Maters, reached up, and tapped her shoulder.

"I can't do it," I whispered, wild-eyed with fear. "I can't sing the solo. I just can't." I was starting to cry.

"Wait right here," she said reassuringly. She turned on her heels, ran over to a boy in my class named Jeffrey, and whispered something in his ear. Jeffrey nodded. Mrs. Maters looked over, smiled, and gave me the "okay" sign. I was off the hook—thank you, Jesus, Mary, and Jeffrey.

I got back to my spot in line just as we were making our grand entrance to the risers. At first I felt self-conscious and shy being so exposed to the audience in my spot in the first row. But I relaxed more and more with each of our numbers. By the end of "Frosty the Snowman," I was starting to think it wasn't so bad up there. During "Rudolph," I caught sight of my parents. *Oops. They're going to wonder what happened.* By halfway through "Jingle Bells," I started thinking I might actually be able to do that solo after all—but it was too late, of course.

When we got to the part of "The Christmas Song" that was supposed to be *my* cue, Jeffrey walked down front to center stage and leaned toward the microphone. I watched with shame as he sang the lines I had practiced in my room for weeks. I'll never forget how I felt as I stood in the background, biting my lip and fighting back tears.

I saw the effect he was having on people. Moms pulled tissues from purses. Dads took photos. Grandparents put arms around grandkids. The moment moved people.

I felt like such a coward. I'd thought that staying hidden in the crowd would keep me safe, but I understood now how wrong I'd been—that trying to be invisible had only led to a different kind of pain. The regret was all-consuming, and it was unbearable.

Let Yourself Be Seen

When I look at a mental snapshot of that moment, I realize that it could have been the story of my whole life. That could be the story of any of our lives if we let fear stop us from sharing what we have to offer.

Yes, there is a cost to being seen: heart palpitations, fear of failure and rejection, the vulnerability of sharing your voice. But there is also a cost to staying hidden: the pain of regret, missed opportunities, not sharing what's inside us and not contributing our gifts to the world.

If we want to reach our full potential, it's imperative that we learn to embrace fear and take risks. We must summon our courage to take those first steps toward sharing what is inside us. How do we do this? A good place to start is to redefine what success means—to decide in advance that the only way to fail is not to try. What if you decided that success equals simply showing up? You never know where that next courageous step might lead you.

An incredible example of the heights we can reach if we're just willing to take a chance comes from Elton John. He may have been one of the most successful musical acts of the 1970s, but in 1967 he was an unknown in the entertainment industry, shy and unsure of himself. That year, however, he answered an advertisement Liberty Records talent scout Ray Williams placed in a music journalism magazine, and everything changed.

John recalled what happened in a 2013 interview with Terry Gross on NPR's *Fresh Air*: "'I can sing and I can write songs,' I said, 'But I can't write lyrics.' And he said, 'Well, here's somebody who writes lyrics.'"

That "somebody" was Bernie Taupin, an aspiring musician who had also responded to the ad—and he and Elton John went on to collaborate on countless hits, including "Rocket Man," "Tiny Dancer," and "Candle in the Wind," which holds the record for the biggest-selling single of all time. As of 2017, Elton John and Bernie Taupin have been creating hit songs together for more than fifty years and have become one of the longest-lasting songwriting duos in music history, and Elton John is one of the top-selling solo artists of all time.

In his interview with Gross, Elton John marveled at what a remarkable turn of events all this was. "That changed my life, that whole thing, that advertisement in the *News-Express*, the fact that I had the courage to do it," he told her. "When I look back now, I can't really understand how I had the courage to do it, knowing how timid I was at that point and how, you know, my self-esteem wasn't very good . . . but . . . I took the leap of faith."

Can you imagine if he hadn't?

Choose Love over Fear

So many of us hesitate at the threshold of our becoming. When we are standing at the precipice of something risky and potent and enlivening, something we really want to do, and we flinch, that flinching is what separates us from a life of full expression and a life that is muted and masked.

Leadership expert Steve Farber has a name for those times when we're standing at the precipice. He calls them OS!Ms, aka "'Oh shit!' moments." All the talent we may have, all the training and effort we put in, won't get us anywhere unless we learn to keep walking forward through our OS!Ms.

That Christmas concert was a big OS!M for me—and instead of walking forward through it, I flinched. I was afraid of failure, so I gave up my solo. Ultimately, though, I think shrinking from that opportunity made me feel worse than I would have felt if I'd tried and failed. Every time we allow fear to prevent us from expressing our gifts, we die a little bit inside. As I watched Jeffrey sing that solo, I understood how much it hurts to let fear hold you back from doing something that deep down you long to do. So, that day, I made a personal vow to myself: In the future, I would show up, no matter how afraid I was. I would never again let my nerves keep me from doing what I loved.

In the years that followed, I mostly kept that promise to myself. Little by little, I leaned a bit further forward into each challenge. Driven by my love and passion for musical theater—and knowing that nothing could feel worse than giving up out of fear—I learned to breathe through the scary moments and forge onward. At sixteen, I began taking private voice lessons to build my confidence and skill set, and when my high school announced that the musical my junior year would be *Annie*, I went to the audition and sang in front of the entire choir room full of fellow hopefuls, even though my heart was racing like a sprinter's the entire time.

Choosing love over fear has its own rewards—the internal benefit we gain from learning that we can trust ourselves to show up and be seen is gift enough. Sometimes we get external rewards as well, though they are never guaranteed and ultimately far less important. As a high school junior, I was a bit long in the tooth to play my dream role of Annie, but being the short kid sometimes has its benefits. I got the lead role—my very first. And I can honestly say that that success, and every one since then, has come as a result of the commitment I made to myself when I was ten.

Engage the Oppressor

A practice of giving voice to what holds you back so your gifts and capacities no longer remain stuck inside you

1. In your journal, describe what holds you back from fully expressing your voice. Give it form. Personify it. Anthropomorphize it. Express it in nature images, color, texture. Begin with "My fear (or silence/stuckness/hesitation) is . . ." What does it look, sound, taste like? What does it do? Don't think, just write, and see where the pen takes you.

 Examples: "My fear is a sixth-grade boy who sticks his foot out and laughs as my face hits the gravel and my bottom lip bleeds."

 "My silence is a desert with no heat, a vast emptiness with no life in sight and no one to hear my cries for help or my song."

2. Turn toward and talk to your oppressor. Ask it what it wants you to know.

 Example: "Why are you keeping me stuck? What do I need to understand?"

 The answer you get might be kind or harsh: "I'm just trying to keep you safe." Or "You don't deserve to be heard."

3. Next, describe the opposite of your fear/silence/stuckness. What qualities are present? What do you see, smell, taste, touch, hear?

 Example: "A golden light like the surface of the sun with beautiful rays pointing in all directions, warm, bright, like luminosity itself. A golden flame like a shield, an angel's harp. It surrounds my body and keeps the darkness from being able to touch me."

4. Turn toward the opposite force and let it speak to you.

Example: "I am the barrier between you and all forces of darkness and shame. I will surround you and fill your body and carry you forward when you're too fearful to move on your own. I am stronger than your ego, your self-image, your susceptibility to criticism. You are a part of me and all that is. Hold tight to me, and I will protect you. You are safe. I've got you. I've got this."

Be True to You

How do we live the most potent expression of who we really are? By opening door after door marked FEAR and walking through. Which, of course, is easier said than done. Within each of us is a battleground between light and darkness, between our desire to be seen and the gravitational force that makes us want to remain invisible. I think there is a huge population of closeted artists. As D. W. Winnicott wrote, "Artists are people driven by the tension between the desire to communicate and the desire to hide." Like a child playing hide-and-seek, covering herself with a pile of leaves but sticking one foot out so she'll be found, our fear causes us to want to stay in the shadows, while another part of us reaches toward the light, knowing that we have something to give.

Part of the reason for this push and pull is that putting yourself out there is frequently painful. The thrill I felt over my achievement when I got the lead role in *Annie* in high school wasn't enough to keep the tears at bay when I saw that someone had gouged out my eyes in the poster of me as Annie that the director had pinned to the hallway bulletin board. I learned quickly that being in the spotlight meant being a target for criticism and cruelty. As the Japanese proverb goes, "The nail that sticks out gets hammered down." But, sensitive as I was to every sling and arrow aimed in my direction, the joy I derived from singing and acting—and from sharing my love for it with my biggest supporter, my dad—made the difficult parts worth enduring.

Being true to yourself is as good a reason as any to stick your neck out. We would tell any one of our friends or children to stay true to their dreams, to follow the quiet yearning in their heart, but we don't always give ourselves the same permission or the same gentle kick in the pants. Yet there is something inside us that is waiting to blossom—and the more we trust that we are enough, the more courage we will have to give life to that which wants to emerge through us.

I certainly don't mean to suggest that taking risks is easy or enjoyable. Sometimes it feels excruciating. Amid all the rejection and heartbreak I experienced in my pursuit of a career in musical theater, I sometimes wished that my desire to perform would simply go away and leave me alone. But it never did. It only got stronger. It felt bigger than me; it was like a giant hand was clasped around my heart, pulling me toward the future. The love I had for that particular form of expression propelled me forward, all the way from Detroit to New York City and into the role that changed my life forever.

Cross the Threshold

Even after landing the role of Christine, I was nowhere near impervious to the criticism of others—or my own self-doubt. Many nights in my dressing room at the Majestic, that fire escape beckoned, and it took everything in me not to succumb to its siren call. Why? I was the leading lady of a huge Broadway hit—the fulfillment of my lifelong dream. I was, by every external marker, a success. And yet, rather than celebrating this achievement, my fear of not being enough just morphed into impostor syndrome.

Confidence wasn't waiting for me in the star dressing room on Broadway, and it isn't waiting at the top of the proverbial ladder, no matter what profession we're in. In fact, successful people often report that "making it" actually intensifies the fear that they'll be found out for the fraud they feel like on the inside. Take Emma Watson, for example, who in a 2013 interview with the website Rookie said, "It's almost like the better I do, the more my feeling of inadequacy actually increases, because I'm just going, *Any moment, someone's going to find out I'm a total fraud, and that I don't deserve any of what I've achieved. I can't possibly live up to what everyone thinks I am and what everyone's expectations of me are.*" And Watson is by no means alone in this. An estimated 70 percent of people experience the feeling that they don't deserve their success and the fear that they are a fraud and everyone knows it.

We hold ourselves back because we don't believe we are worthy of the life we truly desire. Oh, the ways we guilt ourselves! There is so much programming around "Who do you think you are?" We are so afraid others will judge us. But when we commit to leaning into what scares us and saying "yes" even when we're afraid, unseen forces rise up to support us. If you can find the courage to walk through the vulnerability of risk, you'll find that the people you are here to serve are waiting just inside, along with wonders you could never imagine: joy, freedom, fulfillment, and aliveness. Cross the threshold. You're ready.

Questions to Live By

- When was the last time you said no to something you really wanted to do?

- What thoughts held you back?

- Is there a risk you'd like to take now but aren't taking?

- Are the same old fearful, anxious thoughts holding you back? What self-supportive thoughts could you replace them with to give you the courage to move forward?

- Can you make a vow to yourself today to follow the path of love, instead of fear?

Chapter 4:

Rehearse the Positive

Most people have achieved their greatest success just one step beyond their greatest failure.

—Napoleon Hill

When I was about to graduate from Michigan State University, I sat down with my parents to talk about what I was going to do with my communications degree. Fear had kept me from majoring in musical theater, even though it was my passion, but I had spent all of my extra-curricular credits on singing, acting, and dance classes.

My parents knew what was in my heart and, in an act of bravery it took me years to comprehend, encouraged me to take the big risk. "Give it five years," my dad said. "Audition for everything, and if nothing pans out, you can always come back home and figure out plan B."

There were a million reasons I shouldn't have tried to make a living as an actor. There wouldn't have been anything wrong with getting a sensible job and continuing to perform as a hobby. But something—that quiet yearning from within, I suppose—said, *Go*. So off I went to New York City, with my graduation money in my pocket and a five-year plan mapped out in my head.

When I got to the city, I worked every temp job I could find. I answered phones at a social-work office. I passed out mail at the Bank of Tokyo. I shoved my size 6.5 feet into size 6 shoes for a brief stint as a shoe model. And I auditioned—and I'm not talking dozens of auditions; I'm talking hundreds. Yet, despite my best efforts, four and a half years in, all I had to show for those auditions were a handful of roles in out-of-town song-and-dance revues and a mountain of rejections. Mainly what I remember from that time is subsisting on a bagel in the morning and a slice of pizza at night, which allowed me to survive on about $3 a day.

Six months out from my five-year deadline to become a professional singer-actress, I was living on a friend's sofa, I'd maxed out all my credit cards, and it looked like the writing was on the wall: I would soon have to admit to myself and everyone else that I'd failed. I was mentally preparing to pack it in and move back to Michigan.

Then one afternoon, out of nowhere, I got a call from my agent, the late, great Michael Hartig.

"My dear"—he always called me "my dear"—"I have an audition for you for the role of Christine in *The Phantom of the Opera*."

One day, I'm ready to give up, and the next, suddenly, there I am, standing on the stage of the Majestic Theatre in the heart of Times Square underneath that famous giant chandelier. Hal Prince, the brilliant, renowned director (think: the Stephen Spielberg of Broadway), is sitting five rows back with all of the supervisors of the show around him, and it's just me alone on that big stage.

The magnitude of the moment hit me, and I felt like my

fifth-grade self again—trembling with fear. When the pianist started to play, I began to sing the song they had asked for, "Think of Me." Within seconds, my mouth went so dry that my upper lip got stuck to my teeth. Soon I realized my left arm was stuck in midair. I had no idea how it had gotten there, and I could not move it. I had no sensation whatsoever in my legs and wasn't sure it would ever return. I was like a disembodied singing head. But I had practiced every single syllable of that song so many times that it had become muscle memory; I was able to finish it, even hit the high C at the end, before getting the hell out of there.

The next day, my phone rang.

"My dear," Michael said, "you did not get the part." My heart sank. "But they want to give you a job in the ensemble on the national tour."

You may recall the scene where the Phantom takes Christine in a boat and they descend to his underground lair beneath the opera house. There, as he sings the beautiful song "Music of the Night," he pulls the edge of a big black cloth, revealing a mirror image of Christine—a mannequin dressed as a bride. On a big music cue, the mannequin bursts through the mirror in a dramatic gesture that scares Christine so much, she faints.

I was to be the mannequin.

You study acting, singing, and dancing all your life, and you end up playing a dummy—or, as they call her in the show, a "mirror bride." But I wasn't complaining. I was thrilled to be in the cast and overjoyed to finally be earning a paycheck as a performer. I played the dummy and burst through that mirror eight times a week, with gusto, for an entire year on the national tour (the Music Box Company).

Then the actress who played Christine in the Raoul Company (the other national tour) got cast in another show and gave her notice.[3] The role of Christine was opening up again; they were looking for a replacement. The company flew

3. The lovely Sarah Pfisterer, who played Christine in the Raoul Company, left Phantom in 1996 to play Magnolia in the revival of Show Boat on Broadway.

me from the tour to New York to audition for a second time.

There I stood once again on the stage of the Majestic Theatre, underneath that now-familiar giant chandelier. Once again, Hal Prince and the supervisors sat five rows back. For the second time, I was alone on the stage.

The pianist started to play, and I started to sing. This time, I was ready: I had put Vaseline on my upper teeth and gums so my lip could not get stuck. And no way was I going to be frozen in my body this time; on the contrary, I'd decided I was going to show Hal Prince that I could move. Christine is a ballet dancer, so I figured I'd better prove to the creative team that I could be graceful. I gave them big arm gestures, dramatic steps, choreographed movements![4]

It was a disaster.

The next day, Michael called. "My dear, you did not get the part." There was no "but" this time. Instead, Michael just sighed and said softly, "They're going to continue the search for a new Christine."

That's it, I thought. *It's over. I'm never gonna get another chance. I'm forever going to be known as the dummy.*

My return flight got me back to the tour in time for the show that evening. As soon as I arrived at the theater, my friends in the cast rushed over to me, full of smiles, and asked how the audition went. I just shook my head. I didn't trust myself to speak; I was fighting hard to hold back my tears, and I knew that anything could tip the balance.

As Diane Fratantoni, our tour's Christine, began to sing the first notes of "Think of Me" that night—with me right behind her in my ensemble spot—the full weight of all that had just happened hit me. *This is as close to Christine as I'm ever going to get*, I told myself miserably, and I was convinced that it was true. I would never play the part; I was destined to disappoint myself.

As the curtain came down, I prepared to make a beeline

---

4. *I was doing the "Think of Me" choreography without the scarf. To every Christine hopeful, my first piece of advice is this: do not do scarfography at your audition.*

for the exit. But Diane was too fast for me. Before I could make a run for it, she caught my arm and pulled me aside.

"You hang in there," she said, hugging me. She took a step back, put her hands on my shoulders, and looked straight into my bloodshot eyes. "I was a late bloomer. We all get in our own way sometimes. Be gentle with yourself."

I had no idea how to do that.

Change Your Default Setting

We've all heard the platitudes. We know that failure is a necessary step on the path to success. What we don't hear enough about, as a culture, is how to move through the rejection, criticism, disappointment, and self-recrimination that often accompany failure. The temptation is to run away from our feelings, or to flagellate ourselves for not being good enough (I did—and sometimes still do—both). But these methods, as you've undoubtedly learned for yourself by this point in your life, get us nowhere.

I wish we were taught in school how to deal with failure. Can you imagine if we were trained from childhood to practice gratitude and self-compassion when things are hard or when we make a mistake? The default I've turned to many times in my life—and I know I'm not the only one—is to ruminate, ad nauseam, about what went wrong. And there's a reason for this, according to psychologist Homaira Kabir: we are built to take in only the information that dovetails with our mental image of ourselves.

Our tendency to absorb only data that mesh with our self-concept is actually a protective mechanism, according to Homaira; it prevents us from becoming overwhelmed by all the information constantly flying at us. She writes: "When this mental image is less than complimentary, we also get a silent dopamine high (a feeling of *I knew it!*) because the biased information we've taken in fits with our internal narrative. That's why beating down on ourselves is almost addictive—that bitter sweetness of knowing you're unworthy (when you feel ignored), or incompetent (when you face a setback), or unloved (when you make a mistake), and the list goes on."

In other words, it feels good to make yourself feel bad. In the short run, anyway. In the long term, though, ruminating only makes us feel worse. Each time the mind turns over all of the woulda-shoulda-couldas, we carve deeper neural pathways for the negative. We are essentially rehearsing our shortcomings. And this is no way to live—or to grow.

Your Ideal Self

A practice of checking whether your ideal self is grounded in reality*

Take a moment to reflect on these three questions:

1. What is my ideal self? And why is it so? Is it based on early experiences when I was helpless and dependent on the love and appreciation of others to cope with life?

2. Is it realistic? In a world of billions of others, can I truly be the smartest, most beautiful, most loved or faultless person there is? Is there even such a person—or am I, as a human, forgetting that my imperfections are what make me perfect?

3. Is it achievable? Is it aligned with my inherent strengths and weaknesses, or am I desperately pursuing a mirage? Because unless your ideal self is grounded in your unique reality, you will not be able to rise to your highest potential.

*This exercise is excerpted from writing by Homaira Kabir, with her permission.

Be Gentle with Yourself

Self-criticism might be our default after failure and rejection, but self-compassion is a far more skillful and productive response. Studies show that people who engage in self-criticism after a failure learn less from the experience, and the benefits of self-compassion are well documented and plentiful.

Dr. Kristin Neff is a pioneer in the field of self-compassion research. I still remember the compelling self-compassion story she shared at a women's conference I attended in Boulder, Colorado, which she also shared in her 2016 TEDx talk. Her four-year-old son, who has autism, was throwing a gigantic tantrum on a plane in the middle of a flight to England. Everyone, she said, looked at them as if they wished she and her son would die. "He's four years old, he looks normal, people are thinking, *What's wrong with this kid? Why is he acting this way? And what's wrong with his mother? Why can't she control her child?*"

Dr. Neff could have reacted to this situation in a lot of different ways. She could have yelled at her son. She could have crumpled in on herself with shame, joined the other passengers in judging herself unfit as a mother. But she chose a different path. "I knew in that moment the only refuge I had was self-compassion," she said in her talk. "So I put my hands over my heart, and I tried to comfort him, but I was mainly focusing on myself: *This is so hard right now, darling. I'm so sorry you're going through this, but I'm here for you.* And you know what? It got me through. And by allowing myself to be openhearted toward myself, I could remain openhearted to Rowan."

I could fill an entire book with all the research out there that supports the idea Dr. Neff puts forward: that self-compassion has the power to transform. One study, published in the journal *Psychological Science*, found that recently divorced people who spoke compassionately toward themselves adjusted significantly better in the ten months following their divorce than those who spoke more harshly toward themselves. Another survey, this one conducted by the University of California in 2011, found that subjects spent more time studying for a difficult test following an initial failure when they practiced self-compassion. They also reported greater motivation to work on their weaknesses when they practiced self-acceptance.

Suffice it to say, science has spoken: self-compassion is one of the keys to emotional resilience. And this is essential in keeping us moving in the direction of the life we truly want, especially when we run into obstacles along the way.

Dr. Kristin Neff's Self-Compassion Break
A practice of giving ourselves the same kindness and care we'd give to a good friend in a stressful situation*

According to Dr. Neff, self-compassion has three important elements: mindfulness vs. over-identification, common humanity vs. isolation, and self-kindness vs. self-judgment.

Think of a situation in your life that is difficult, that is causing you stress. Call the situation to mind, and see if you can actually feel the stress and emotional discomfort in your body. Now, say to yourself:

1. **This is a moment of suffering.** That's mindfulness. Other options include:
   - This hurts.
   - Ouch.
   - This is stress.

2. **Suffering is a part of life.** That's common humanity. Other options include:
   - Other people feel this way.

- I'm not alone.
- We all struggle in our lives.

Now, put your hands over your heart; feel the warmth of your hands and the gentle touch of your hands on your chest. Or adopt any soothing touch that feels right for you.

3. **May I be kind to myself.** Ask yourself, "What do I need to hear right now to express kindness to myself?" Is there a phrase that speaks to you in your particular situation? Consider these:
    - May I give myself the compassion that I need.
    - May I learn to accept myself as I am.
    - May I forgive myself.
    - May I be strong.
    - May I be patient.

This practice can be used any time of day or night, and will help you remember to evoke the three aspects of self-compassion when you need it most.

*Used with permission from Dr. Kristin Neff.

Make Gratitude Your Guide

In her book *Mindset: The New Psychology of Success*, Carol Dweck discusses the importance of having a "growth mindset" versus a "fixed mindset." A fixed mindset, she explains, assumes that we are who we are, and we are incapable of changing in any meaningful way. A growth mindset, in contrast, "is based on the belief that your basic qualities are things you can cultivate through your efforts" and frames failure "not as evidence of unintelligence but as a heartening springboard for growth and for stretching our existing abilities." And this is important, she says, because when you think your intelligence, personality, and everything else about you are unchangeable, it makes you feel like you have to prove yourself constantly—a belief that traps you in a binary cycle of winning and failing, with no potential for learning and evolving. But when you believe you're capable of growth, you can adopt a longer view of the situation at hand and begin to see even failure as an opportunity.

Essentially, what Dweck is saying is that if we truly want to learn from our experiences, we must resist the urge to wallow in our feelings of failure. Instead, we need to learn to investigate our feelings, thoughts, and sensations. Because once we've identified the good and accepted the bad, we can begin to rehearse new thought patterns—and in doing so, we can actually change our brains for the better, learn from our mistakes, and improve our future performance.

The best vehicle we can use to move out of resistance and into acceptance and serenity is gratitude. We can rehearse feeling thankful and make a daily habit of noticing what is abundant about our current situation, instead of what is lacking. We open ourselves to growth by practicing self-compassion and gratitude and by asking ourselves, *What helpful information can be gleaned here? What can I learn from this?* There may be moments when the negative voices in our heads are loud, but if we can learn to be a good friend to ourselves, we will become more resilient.

I learned this lesson after bombing my second Christine audition. For the first couple of weeks afterward, night after night, I agonized over how I had blown such an incredible opportunity not once but twice. I was so angry at myself, and so disappointed. I became more and more disgusted with myself with each passing day.

One night, I was alone in my hotel room and I couldn't sleep. I kept replaying the audition in my mind and cringing at how stupid I'd been. I sat up in bed and got out my journal to try to clear my head: "I blew it. It's over. I've hit the glass ceiling now, proven to them that I'm incapable of playing the lead role. This is as far as I'm ever going to get." My pen kept moving, bleeding all of my heartache onto the page.

Then I flipped back to some older entries and saw one I'd written a year earlier, when I was working at the Bank of Tokyo. My dream at that time had been to simply get to sing and act for a living. I was actually already living the dream I'd had only one year prior. How had I lost sight of how far I had come?

I flipped to a new page in my journal and started writing down all of the things I had to be grateful for: my job, my family and friends, that I was able to do something I loved every day, that I got to share the stage with such incredible people. By the time I was finished, I felt lighter.

From then on, that was my ritual: every night before bed, I filled my journal with all of the things I had to be grateful for. Within a matter of days, I felt my mood lift.

Writing nightly gratitudes is a practice I continue to this day. When things are difficult or I've failed in some way, I sometimes ramp up to twice a day and write what I'm grateful for in the morning and in the evening. I've found that bookending my day by focusing on the positive helps me shift out of self-pity and negativity and gives me a greater sense of agency in my life.

Suspend Your Disbelief

Talk to anyone who has achieved success in their field—chances are, they've seen a helluva lot of failure. *Chicken Soup for the Soul* was rejected 144 times—and then, when Jack Canfield and Mark Victor Hansen finally found a publisher, it was a tiny self-help press based in Deerfield Beach, Florida, that offered them no advance and said they'd be lucky to sell 20,000 copies. When Canfield and Hansen said they wanted to sell 150,000 copies by Christmas, their publisher laughed. Today, the series has sold more than 500 million copies worldwide. J. K. Rowling was told not to quit her day job. Babe Ruth led the American League in strikeouts five times and had struck out a total of 1,330 times by the end of his career. Oprah Winfrey was publicly fired from her first television job as an anchor in Baltimore for getting "too emotionally invested in her stories."

I never tire of these tales.

Actors know rejection intimately. We hear "no" dozens, if not hundreds, of times before we hear "yes." Still, we stand in those cattle-call lines before the sun rises. We persevere out of love—and maybe a touch of madness. As actor Will Smith once said, "There's a certain delusional quality that all successful people have to have. You have to believe something different can happen."

Doing this is a form of what poet-critic Samuel Taylor Coleridge called "the willing suspension of disbelief." It's something we've all engaged in at some point, usually without even thinking about it. We do it when we're reading a book or watching a movie or play. Although we know in our logical, rational minds that what we're reading or seeing is not happening in reality, we willingly buy into the author's world. It's a powerful trick of the mind—and it's one we can apply to our everyday life. It's especially useful if we've recently experienced rejection or failure while in pursuit of a goal. Sometimes, the suspension of disbelief is all it takes to get you back on your feet.

So, the next time you hear yourself saying, "It's never going to happen for me"—when you've tried your best and your best wasn't good enough—remember that you cannot see what might be right around the corner. Try suspending your disbelief. It may very well be that when it all seems like it's over and you're ready to call it quits, you're actually standing at the threshold of the biggest opportunity of your life.

That's precisely what happened to me.

After my second failed audition for Christine, I was convinced a third opportunity would not present itself. But just a couple of weeks later, I got another call from Michael.

"My dear," he said, his voice bubbling with excitement, "they still haven't found a new Christine. They want to bring you back and give you . . . One. Last. Chance."

Questions to Live By

- How do you treat yourself when you make a mistake?

- How do you treat someone you love when they make a mistake?

- Can you practice self-compassion when you make a mistake, fail, or experience rejection?

- What is abundant in your life today that wasn't true only a year ago?

- Is there something you don't think will ever happen for you? What would it feel like to suspend your disbelief for a minute, an hour, a day?

Chapter 5:

Find Your Field of Power

The creative process can be a means of discovering a voice for the you inside you—the tender, secret you—that has long been buried under a mountain of expectation.

—Anita Jesse

When Michael told me Hal Prince wanted to bring me back for one last audition for Christine, I was ecstatic . . . and terrified. I had already failed twice. What was to prevent me from failing a third time?

I couldn't botch it again.

I'd been tripping over my own feet, and I knew it. At the first audition, I had been stiff and unnatural. At the second audition, I had been artificial and contrived. Both approaches were clearly manifestations of my own insecurity and desperation to prove my worth.

One of my first acting teachers used to say, "The most important thing about a performance is that it is truthful and alive." I thought about this as I prepared for my third audition. *What do I have to do in order to be truthful and alive?* I asked myself. The answer was obvious: *I need to be present and authentic.* The first two auditions had felt like out-of-body experiences to me; I barely remembered them. I certainly hadn't been present. And as far as authenticity went, there I was, auditioning for a show about a guy wearing a mask, and it was very clear to me that I had donned a sort of mask of my own when I'd walked into those auditions. The first time, it was a mask of fear that prevented me from fully expressing myself; the second time, it was a mask of overcompensation that led me to layer on a bunch of external stuff. Why? Because I was trying to cover up the one thing I feared the most: that I just wasn't good enough.

So I began to think, *How can I show up differently the next time?* Luckily, I had a work session with *Phantom*'s supervisors a few days before my third audition. I am forever indebted to Peter von Mayrhauser and Kristen Blodgette for giving it to me straight. They saw that I was pushing and told me to stop. "Don't even wear a dress next time," Peter said. I'd taken great pains to find dresses that evoked Christine without being too literal and I'd worn them to the first two auditions. "Wear something like what you have on now," he said. I was wearing simple black pants and a black turtleneck sweater—very un-Christine![5] "It's all already there," Kristen said. They were giving me permission to bring more of my true self into the audition room. But how could I do that when the stakes were so high? I decided to go back to basics.

In acting training, we're taught to consider the inner monologue of the character we're playing. We learn to focus not only on the words in the script but also on what

---

5. *A note to young actors: Please don't take this as a sign that you should start wearing all black to every audition. It is often advisable to dress in a manner that evokes the character you're auditioning for, as long as you don't lean into costume territory.*

the character is *thinking* as she speaks those words. I did this with Christine, but I realized that I needed to also do it for myself. I began looking at my own internal monologue. What was I saying to myself going into those first two auditions? *I've got to get the part! I have to be the best! I need to nail it!* Obviously, that hadn't worked for me. So I decided to try a completely different approach and flip the script on my inner monologue: *I'm not here to get the part. I don't have to be perfect. I'm not here to prove anything.*

This audition took place not at the Majestic but in Hal Prince's Rockefeller Center office. Only one other girl was there, and she went first. I could hear her voice through the door as she sang "Think of Me." It was beautiful. Flawless. The cadenza at the end sounded effortless. I looked around at the Tony awards on shelves and posters from the shows Mr. Prince had produced or directed, going back decades, and felt the old, familiar cinder block of unworthiness in my stomach. I took a deep breath and let it out slowly.

The other girl came out, and I went in.

As the pianist began playing the intro to "Think of Me," I felt my anxiety rise up, and the urge to overcompensate—to try too hard—once again came over me. This time, though, I allowed the feelings to be there. *May I be present*, I thought. *May I be authentic. And may I give my whole heart to this moment.*

With those thoughts in mind, I approached the scene and song with a lighter touch. Christine is nervous when she begins singing "Think of Me," I reminded myself, so my nerves were a gift. There was nothing I needed to layer on top of them; what I really needed to do was strip away everything else, including my desire to prove myself or get the part. Christine's confidence builds throughout the song, and as I sang from the most honest place I could access within me, so did mine.

From a vocal standpoint, the performance I delivered

that day wasn't my strongest—not a perfect ten. But in the song, and in the scene I read after it, I used what was real. I let myself be spontaneous and make unexpected choices in the moment. That openness helped me to find Christine's heartbeat within my own chest. She was uncomfortable in the spotlight. It took time for her to find her voice and confidence. I couldn't have auditioned for a character more similar to me if I'd written her myself. For the first time, I felt emotionally connected during the audition.

A week later, I got a call from Michael.

"My dear," he said, "are you sitting down?"

My first phone call after I hung up with Michael was to my parents. My dad went for a drive and started honking the horn and yelling out the window at strangers, "My daughter just got the lead in *The Phantom of the Opera*!"

Connect from the Heart

Here's what I now know after standing on the stage as Christine more than a thousand nights in a row: *Phantom* has survived and thrived for as long as it has because it touches people—because it has an emotional impact on its audience. Of course people love the beautiful music, the dazzling set, and the opulent costumes, but as the brilliant Ron Bohmer once said in an interview about the show, "You can always spend a lot of money and drop a chandelier on people, but if you can break their hearts, then you've got something." Just as emotional connection played a role in my winning the role of Christine, emotional connection has undoubtedly played a role in making *Phantom* the most profitable entertainment enterprise of all time.

Advertisers spend billions of dollars every year trying to make an emotional connection with consumers. Why? Because countless studies have shown that we humans make decisions based on emotions. Neurologist Antonio

Damasio's research has shown that patients with damage to the part of the prefrontal cortex that processes emotions often struggle with making decisions, even routine ones like what to eat for lunch. Damasio's findings are an extreme demonstration of a fact that most of us already intuitively know: we may use our heads to gather information, but our hearts ultimately dictate our choices. Our ability to make an emotional connection with others, then, affects both our internal world and our external success, including our bottom line.

I learned a great deal about emotional connection and bottom-line results from the show I was blessed to be a part of for ten years. *Phantom*, after all, has been seen by 140 million people around the world, and its worldwide box office earnings are upwards of $6 billion. It has outgrossed even the most successful films in history—more than *Titanic*, *Avatar*, *Star Wars*, and *E.T.* It has been translated into fifteen languages and has played thirty-five countries around the world. This is not just another Broadway musical; *The Phantom of the Opera* is a global, iconic brand, and it has reached these heights because it touches something raw and vulnerable in the people who come to see it.

In her wonderful book *Daring Greatly*, Brené Brown defines vulnerability as uncertainty, risk, and emotional exposure. These three ingredients are required not only to create an authentic performance as an actor but also to create a fulfilling life. Uncertainty: you don't know what's going to happen. Risk: you're going to show up even though things may not go the way you want them to. Emotional exposure: you let others see your heart. We can all feel when someone is being disingenuous or putting on a show. When someone has armored up, it sends a subtle signal that pushes others away. But when someone is being sincere and authentic, there's a tendency to lean toward that person. It is only when we are open, when something real in me touches something real in you, that we make a genuine connection. In that third audition for Hal, Peter, and Kristen, I finally allowed myself to be vulnerable, to drop the mask and show them something real, and that's what made all the difference.

We are in the age of authenticity. As Seth Godin said in *Leap First: Creating Work That Matters*, "We are leaving the industrial economy and entering the connection economy. What people are paying for and flocking to and talking about is connection. What we have to do to win in the connection economy is emotional labor."

In other words, we have to be all in from the heart.

I am not suggesting that vulnerability is a magic formula for getting what we want. But it is the key to getting something deeper, truer, and more lasting. We get the experience of connection. We get to stand out in the open, unmasked, sharing who we are. And when we do that, the importance of the outcome pales in comparison.

Write a new inner monologue or mantra to help center yourself before you walk into vulnerable situations. For example: *I'm not here to be perfect . . . I'm here to be present.* Or: *Nothing to prove, No one to be. Enough to be here. Enough to be me.*

Right Size

I recently asked a casting director friend of mine, "What's the biggest mistake you see in auditions?"

"It's one of two things," she said. "Either people come in apologizing or they go over the top."

I cringed. I had, of course, been guilty of both. At the first audition, my demeanor had been apologetic. My inner monologue—*I'm not good enough to be here. This is too big for me. Please don't see me*—had caused me to shrink. At the second audition, I had gone way too big. Believing *I'm not good enough* had led me to overcompensate. And I have to admit, I recognize that I have a tendency to do the same thing in life. When I walk into a situation that feels too big for me, that feels intimidating, I sometimes shrink, hide, or deflate myself in some way—my default since childhood. When someone is critical of me, on the other hand, I feel the urge to inflate or puff myself up.

If you're not an actor or singer, you may think that your work experiences and mine have very little in common. However, I've found that no matter what a person does for a living, they encounter many of the same challenges actors face. We all have to take risks and sometimes feel anxious or fear we're inadequate in the midst of them. Maybe you have to give a presentation at work or you're put in charge of a team; maybe you're given a big project you weren't expecting and a deadline you're not sure you can meet. Business coach and author Kat Koppett writes in her book *Training to Imagine*, "The feelings improvisers [performers] can have onstage—self-consciousness, pressure to get things right, not wanting to make a fool of themselves—are different only in intensity, not in kind, [from] the pressures that many of us feel most of the time."

"Many of us" is right. A staggering number of Americans not only feel these pressures but feel them *acutely*. According to the Anxiety and Depression Association of America (ADAA), anxiety affects 40 million Americans over the age of 18 (roughly 18 percent of the nation's population) each year. The ADAA further notes that of those 40 million people, almost 7 million of them suffer from generalized anxiety disorder (GAD), 15 million suffer from social anxiety disorder, 14.8 million suffer from major depressive disorder, and 7.7 million are affected by post-traumatic stress disorder. That's one in seven people, all told.

How about you? When you're in a high-pressure situation—a meeting with someone who intimidates you, or when you have to give an important presentation—what happens? Do you play it safe and freeze up? Do you push too hard and come off as desperate? What can you do to create the conditions that would allow you to bring your *real* self into those high-pressured situations? How can you be your most open, authentic self, even when you're nervous?

Conversation Observation

A practice of observing yourself when you are most "you," so you can bring your authentic essence to high-pressure situations

1. The next time you're talking to someone you feel completely confident around—maybe it's your spouse or your best friend—bring up a topic you're passionate about or a story you want to share with them.

2. As you're talking, practice dual awareness: Let one part of your mind be the witness to your experience. Observe your authentic communication style. Begin to notice, *This is my tone when I'm confident and passionate. This is the way I gesture. This is what my body language is like.*

3. The next time you're in a high-stakes situation, see if you can inhabit those same qualities and characteristics. You are rehearsing being relaxed, open, and thoroughly yourself so that in high-stakes situations you have a point of reference that can help you re-create your authentic communication style.

Stand in Your Field of Power

Tibetans have a word, *wangthang*, that means "authentic presence." It literally translates to "field of power." In order to "bring about authentic presence," says Tibetan teacher Chögyam Trungpa Rinpoche—in order to occupy your own field of power—"you have to be without clinging." He further explains that "the cause or the virtue that brings about authentic presence is emptying out and letting go."

We can practice dropping our drivenness and loosening our fists. Instead of trying to be perfect or to control outcomes, we can bring a quality of surrender and relaxed focus that allows room for grace. The trick is to notice when we're beginning to cling to our desired outcome. Here are some signs to look for.

You know you've stepped outside your field of power when you are:

- seeking approval or validation from others
- overly results-oriented
- evaluating your worth by external markers (how many dollar signs are in your bank account, how many "likes" you get or Twitter followers you have)
- always chasing after something bigger and better, spurred by a feeling of not having enough

You're solidly standing in your field of power when you:

- seek expressiveness out of love
- enjoy the process, the craft, of whatever it is you're doing
- have a background sense of deliberate action, fueled by creative energy moving through you
- immerse yourself in doing something for its own sake

- have the underlying sense that good enough is good enough, independent of external results, reactions, "success," or "failure"

One of my favorite tools for empowerment is listening to Paraliminals. Created by Learning Strategies, Paraliminals are meditative audio recordings that help you activate your whole mind, your whole brain, every time you listen. The messages don't reprogram you; they teach you on a deep level how to respond differently to what's going on in your world and help you cultivate the inner resources you need to be at your best.

Here's how it works: In the recording, you hear a voice in each ear speaking to different sides of your brain; the left voice generally weaves metaphors for the creative right brain, and the right voice generally leads you through logical change processes for the analytical left brain. The multiple voices soothe and relax. The goal is not to try to listen to the voices but rather to enjoy the flow and rhythm.

My favorite is the Peak Performance Paraliminal*; I listen to it before any performance I'm nervous about. I've been stunned by its efficacy.

* Download the Peak Performance Paraliminal and other freely offered resources at **www.sandrajoseph.com/bookgifts**.

When we drop the mask and trust that we're enough, our essence becomes visible. That's when a performance, whether onstage or in life, comes alive.

On the surface, my audition journey makes for a great story because I got the part in the end. In a deeper sense, though, the real gift of that entire experience was that it brought me to a place where I was able to stand in my field of power—and that changed my life in far more important ways than getting to play a leading role in a musical.

Questions to Live By

- Can you describe a time when you played small or deflated yourself?

- Can you describe a time when you overcompensated or inflated yourself?

- Can you describe a time when you inhabited your authentic presence? How did you know you were standing in your field of power?

- Under what circumstances do you feel most yourself?

*Shaun Cassidy tee, Donny and Marie dolls—
and an* Annie *ticket in my stocking*

My first leading role at sixteen

Backstage at the Pantages Theatre in Hollywood

One of my favorite costumes

With Ron Bohmer as the Phantom

Dad in his acting days

Proud papa outside the Pantages in Hollywood

With the record breaking cast, January 9, 2006

As of this writing, this iconic photo with Howard McGillin has been outside the Majestic Theatre for twelve years.

With Mom, Dad, and Monica at Waldorf Astoria gala after
Phantom's *record-breaking performance*

Celebrating with Dad

With John Cudia as Raoul

Gondola ride with Hugh Panaro as the Phantom

With Howard McGillin

Waking up in the Phantom's lair

Chapter 6:

Value Your Fellow Players

Do your little bit of good where you are; it's those little bits of good put together that overwhelm the world.

—Archbishop Desmond Tutu

I played Christine for two years all across the United States on the national tour, and then, in late 1997, I was invited to join the Broadway cast. My Broadway debut was January 29, 1998, just after *Phantom*'s ten-year anniversary. Thirty of my family members had flown from Michigan to New York for my opening-night performance. I had an appointment with my voice teacher earlier that day so he could help me warm up, and I invited my dad to join me at the lesson—partly because I knew he would get a kick out of the session itself, and partly because my teacher had let me know that Glenn Close was coming for a lesson right before mine, so she would be there. I thought it would be exciting for my dad to meet such a big star.

Before we went to the studio that day, I lectured my dad about not embarrassing me in front of Glenn Close, telling him to act natural when he met her, cautioning him against making a scene. For my part, I planned to be cool and collected, as if I met stars of the stage and screen all the time. But the minute I saw her in the flesh, all of my intentions flew out the window and I did enough gushing over her to embarrass both myself *and* my dad—telling her how I had recently seen her in *Sunset Boulevard*, how wonderful she had been in it, and how moved I had been by the lovely curtain speech she'd given at the performance, in which she thanked *everyone*, including the electrician and the box office staff.

My voice teacher finally saved me from myself by cutting in and telling Ms. Close that I was making my own debut on Broadway that night. She was extraordinarily gracious as she wished me a broken leg.

Hours later, I walked into the Majestic Theatre, my body humming with nervous energy. When he saw me, Craig, the production stage manager, caught my eye and waved me over.

"Everything okay?" I asked.

"Everything's fine," he assured me. "I just wanted to say I hope you can walk around in there!" He gestured good-naturedly toward my dressing room.

Confused, I followed the gesture and walked through the door—and found that the dressing room was overflowing with flowers.

Overcome by the sheer quantity of blossoms in the room, I did the only thing I could think to do: I began to inspect the notes attached to each bouquet. Tears filled my eyes as I read the names on the cards. All of my family had sent bouquets; so had friends; so had colleagues from the national tour; so had producer Cameron Mackintosh; so had Hal Prince. The only bouquet whose source I couldn't determine was a huge bunch of gorgeous white flowers; there was a card attached, but I couldn't make out the name scribbled on it. I continued to stare at it, and suddenly the letters took shape: "Glenn Close." The bouquet was from *Glenn Close*. I couldn't believe it. I was floating on air when I took the stage that night.

Embrace Vicarious Joy

Many of us know the word "schadenfreude"—taking pleasure in another's pain—but not enough of us know the word *mudita*. It's a word I've only recently become familiar with. *Mudita* is a Sanskrit word that means "vicarious joy" or "taking pleasure in other people's good fortune"—essentially, it's the polar opposite of "schadenfreude." When things are going well, delighting in someone else's well-being is like sharing a delicious meal: the pleasure is doubled because it is shared. But what I've noticed is that *mudita* is perhaps most useful when things are not going so well. When we are suffering or in pain, just knowing that someone else is experiencing something positive can broaden our view of the whole of life and give us perspective when we most need it. The universe isn't filled with darkness just because things may be dark where we are. There are always points of light, and we need their brilliance to find our way.

Much of the time, these points of light in the darkness are the loved ones who seem to know the way we're meant to go even when we feel utterly lost—the kindhearted souls who are present with us when we need support or who listen without judgment when we don't know if we can go on. Like when I was in my pre-*Phantom* years, trying to make it in New York, and so broke I could barely afford to eat, and my dad gave me $500 I knew he didn't have to keep me going. Or when my sister, Monica, gave me money so I could buy Christmas presents for our family. Or when my friends Rex and Gene let me live on their pullout sofa rent-free for months and treated me like I was a visitor from the Royal Family the entire time. Or when my vocal coach gave me lessons on credit because I didn't have the money to pay him. Each person was a teacher to me.

So, yes, many times those points of light that reveal themselves to us are friends and loved ones. Sometimes, though, they are perfect strangers—generous souls who lend us their support or extend us some unexpected kindness out of their own goodwill.

Taking an interest in others—genuinely, with no agenda or secret hope for personal gain—is such a beautiful way to be in the world. Glenn Close could have written me off as a starstruck nobody the day we met. Instead, she took the time to wish me well and send me flowers on the biggest night of my life. I was humbled by her generosity and other-centeredness; it made me want to emulate her behavior. And as I began to do this more and more, I learned a lesson we all learn when we start extending ourselves for the benefit of others: ultimately, showing kindness to others is a way to show kindness to ourselves.

Psychologists have produced plenty of data to prove that doing good for others is great for all of us. A study published in the *Review of General Psychology* in 2005, for example, found that participants who performed five acts of kindness every week for six weeks saw a significant boost in happiness. Another study, published in the American Psychological Association journal *Emotion* in 2016, found that participants who were prompted to do acts of kindness experienced increases in positive emotions and decreases in negative emotions, whereas those assigned to engage in self-focused behavior did not—suggesting that although people seeking happiness may be tempted to "treat" themselves, they're more likely to succeed if they opt to treat someone else instead.

Loving-kindness meditation (LKM) is a practice derived from the Buddhist tradition that involves mentally sending goodwill, kindness, and warmth toward others—and toward the most difficult people of all: ourselves. Psychologist Barbara Frederickson has done a lot of wonderful research on the benefits of LKM. One study she conducted, published in 2008, found that, over time, practicing LKM increased participants' daily experiences of positive emotions—which, in turn, led to increased mindfulness, purpose in life, and social support, and decreased illness symptoms.

What does all this research tell us? We will be happier and healthier if we bring careful attention to every interaction we have with other people, whether we know them personally or not. Instead of engaging in gossip, we may want to find the good in others and race to let them know when someone has said kind things about them behind their back. Maybe we will go out of our way to acknowledge people who might feel ignored or show appreciation to people whose efforts might be overlooked.

I recently saw one of these small kindnesses in action when I was shopping in a huge furniture store. A young woman was mopping the floors, and an elderly woman stopped to congratulate her on how sparkling clean everything was.

The young woman lit up. "I've been at it all day," she said. "I was supposed to be off at 5:00 p.m., but I'm staying late to get it done. Thank you for noticing!"

Connection Reflection

A practice of inwardly connecting with the people you love and extending that love outward through loving-kindness meditation.

Meditation can feel like a chore sometimes, another thing on your to-do list that you may not get to in a day and then judge yourself for skipping. LKM transformed my own relationship with meditation. (Full disclosure: there were actually two things that contributed to the shift for me—practicing LKM and simultaneously using an app created by HeartMath called Inner Balance.) It turned what used to be a "should" into something I actually look forward to doing. It isn't boring! You get to contemplate the positive qualities in people and wish them well. I usually start out with a goal of practicing for only ten minutes, but it feels so wonderful that I often end up staying with it far longer.

It's no surprise that research shows a multitude of physiological benefits to this practice. When I read Barbara Fredrickson's research, I found it so exciting that it became a huge motivator for me to start doing LKM daily. Here's my slight variation on LKM, a practice I call Connection Reflection. This practice works for me, but please feel free to play around with the steps and use your own phrases to see what works best for you:

1. Sit comfortably and close your eyes. Breathe a little more deeply than you normally would. Imagine your breath going into and out of your heart area.

2. Bring to mind someone who cares about you. It need not be a perfect relationship, but think of someone who truly cares about your well-being. Let the feeling of being cared about warm your heart.

3. Now bring to mind someone you love. Think about the good qualities that person embodies. Silently wish them well, using your own version of the four classic phrases of LKM, staying with each phrase for one full in-and-out breath. Here are the phrases I use:
   - May you be peaceful and happy.
   - May you be healthy and filled with vitality.
   - May you be safe from internal and external harm.
   - May you live with ease and joy.

4. Continue the practice with other people you love or anyone you know who could use some positive thoughts. Next, think of a neutral person—the cashier at the grocery store, perhaps. Wish them the above.

5. Wish yourself each of the four phrases.

It's important to include yourself in LKM. You can begin with yourself, if you like, but you may find it easier to "warm up" your heart by sending loving-kindness to people you care about first.

You can continue wishing the four phrases to as many people as you like. Consider ending by zooming out and wishing that your entire community, state, country, or even the planet or all sentient beings will be happy, healthy, safe, and peaceful.

Prioritize Your Relationships

Simply stated, other people matter. Relationships with family, friends, mentors, and, yes, even strangers are paramount to our success in all the ways that make life worth living.

Decades' worth of data have proven this idea true. One of the most compelling bodies of research is Harvard's Grant and Glueck studies, which tracked the physical and emotional well-being of two populations—456 poor men from Boston and 268 male graduates from Harvard's classes of 1939–1944—over the course of seventy-five years, ending in 2014. What they found, according to Robert Waldinger, a Harvard professor of psychology and the director of the center behind the study, is that the single most important factor in individual happiness is not what kind of car you can afford or how much power you wield at work. It's how much time you spend with people you care for.

"The clearest message that we get from this seventy-five-year study is this: good relationships keep us happier and healthier. Period," Waldinger said in a 2015 TEDx talk.

Gather Your Spiritual Support
A practice of actively becoming more aware of the many ways in which you are supported

1. Sit quietly and close your eyes.

2. Feel how the surface you are sitting on is supporting you. Notice how your musculoskeletal structure is supporting you. As you breathe, feel how all the air you need is there for you.

3. Bring to mind someone who cares about you. It may not be a perfect relationship, but think of a person who cares about your well-being. Let the feeling of being cared for fill your heart. Call to mind anyone—whether you know them personally or not—who would encourage you to live the truest expression of who you are. Think of ancestors, spiritual leaders, counselors or therapists, authors, mentors, teachers, or anyone else who gives you a sense of being supported toward the life you want.

4. Imagine them standing in a circle around you. In your mind's eye, look around the circle and make eye contact with each person. What does each one have to say to you?

5. Spend a few minutes with your journal, writing down anything that these inner-support team members shared.

Invest in Yourself

When we live an other-centered life, the benefits are plentiful. There are times when it's important to focus on ourselves as well, however. Sometimes we need to invest in ourselves by seeking out people who can help us reach our goals, with the understanding that cultivating our talents and passions is not a selfish pursuit.

I had much to learn when I first came to New York after college, but I did know enough to understand that if I wanted to excel, I'd need to work with master-level teachers. So I sought them out. I studied with artists whose talent was awe-inspiring. I worked diligently on what they taught me; I practiced and absorbed myself in what I was learning. I took private lessons and workshops I could not afford. I ran out of money repeatedly, but I still invested in myself, working long hours at minimum-wage jobs so I could eat, sleep, and breathe the singing, acting, and dance training I was receiving from each gifted individual with whom I worked.

I missed out on a lot of movies and dinners with friends. But the training I received from the support team I built for myself—the team I scrimped and saved in order to pay for—prepared me for the life-changing opportunity that was headed my way. My loved ones gave me the courage to pursue my dreams and the mentors in whom I invested my hard-earned money helped me cultivate the skills I needed to make it to Broadway. I still take voice lessons and work with performance and business coaches to this day.

Personal and professional development deserves to be prioritized. Your dreams matter. I am not suggesting you max out your credit cards and skip meals, the way I did in those early years, but I do believe in cutting corners where we must so that we can invest in coaching and classes that fuel our creativity, passion, inner resources, and skill set. It is not selfish to spend time and money to develop the gifts, talents, and capabilities that lie within you. An investment in yourself is also an investment in the people you love, because when you invest in your passions, your aliveness becomes infectious.

My friend Steve Farber (yep—the same one who coined the phrase OS!M) loves music. He took up guitar as a teenager and soon began writing songs. He says that singing and playing guitar were practically all he did in high school. He's now a very successful business owner, and for a long time, music took a backseat to his work. Lately, though, he has rediscovered his passion and started singing and playing again, and he loves it so much that he has decided to create a whole album of his original songs. He goes into the recording studio in a few weeks—a project that will cost him a sizable amount of time and money. Time that he will never get back. Money that he may never recoup. But he isn't concerned about the time and he isn't doing it for the money. He's investing in himself because for him, music is life-giving.

My husband, Ron, and I had dinner recently with Steve and his wife, Veronica. She told me she loves seeing Steve so excited—that his happiness is making her so happy. Ron and I felt it, too. Steve's enthusiasm was palpable. His joy lifted all of us up.

Cherish Your Champions

The most significant thing that happened the night I wrote about in Chapter 2—when I was eight years old and saw *Annie* for the first time—was not watching the musical itself, or the fact that I gave voice to my ambition in the car on the way home. It was what happened afterward.

"I know what I want to do with my life," I said. It felt like my heart was tumbling out of my mouth. As soon as I uttered the words, my father met my gaze in the rearview mirror. In his eyes, I saw a whole galaxy of you-can-do-it-ness. He didn't say anything—but he didn't need to. I knew he believed in me. And more importantly, I knew he loved me no matter what.

It occurs to me now that every good thing that's ever happened in my career can be traced back to that one moment: sitting in a light blue Buick headed toward Harvard Street in Detroit and looking into that particular pair of hazel eyes in the rearview mirror. If they had shown anything less than wholehearted belief in what, to another parent, might have seemed an impossible dream, the entire trajectory of my life might have changed.

In the end, no one gets far without *some* kind of support, whether it be from family, friends, mentors, or even strangers. We need each other. Nobody makes it alone.

Questions to Live By

- Are you investing in developing yourself so you can move powerfully toward your dreams and goals?

- Who are your cheerleaders and champions?

- Is there someone in your life who encourages you to go for it?

- Are you being a champion for someone else?

- Is there someone in whose eyes you see reflected the "you" of your highest potential— someone who will love you no matter if you succeed or fail?

Chapter 7:

Keep Your Performance Fresh

The real voyage of discovery consists not in seeking new landscapes, but in having new eyes.

—Marcel Proust

In a scene in the musical called "The Journey," the Phantom takes Christine on a gondola ride to his underground lair beneath the Paris Opera. Christine describes "swirling mist upon a vast, glassy lake." She calls the Phantom's lair a "world of unending night", she speaks repeatedly of "darkness." It's a haunting scene—and it's one I always loved playing.

There was one moment in particular that I can still feel in my bones. When the gondola ride begins, I am facing upstage, looking at the Phantom. But as we move downstage toward the audience, Christine, curious to see where the Phantom is taking her, turns and looks outward, facing the audience. The audience needs to see through Christine's eyes that the place is massive and creepy, yet enticing. So, each night, when I turned around in the gondola, although what I was actually seeing as I looked up and out into the darkened theater were the red EXIT signs and the sconces along the walls of the Majestic, I let my imagination run wild. One night, the Phantom's lair was the size of a football field, the walls oozing with mud. I might "see" a snake off in the distance or rats crawling along the shore. Another night, I might turn my head and see a corridor off to the side with what appeared to be a tree in a distant corner. Was it a real tree or an old opera set piece?

I also drew on some of my other senses. What scents were in the Phantom's lair? Always, there was the smell of candle wax, but I might imagine a musty odor or the smell of rotting wood, a swampy scent or a smoky one. The air might feel humid and sticky or dry and chilling.

No matter what I imagined seeing out there, I would soon turn back toward the magnetic force that drew my attention above all else: the man in the white mask. Looking into the eyes of the actors I was blessed to perform opposite usually gave me all I needed to stay engaged in the scene. But there were times—plenty of them—when my body was in that gondola and my mind was off somewhere else that had nothing to do with the Phantom or his lair.

The number one question I am asked when people find out I played Christine more than a thousand times is, "How did you keep it fresh night after night?" Honestly, even when I was nudging my imagination into overdrive, it wasn't easy. More than once, in the middle of a song, I caught myself making a to-do list in my head or thinking about what I was going to eat after the performance. Being a part of a long-running show like *Phantom* is like having a recurring dream: the same thing happens over and over and over again. The difference is, with a recurring dream you're just a passive observer, but when you're onstage you have to be fully engaged and present moment by moment, night after night. As much as I loved playing the role, singing the same songs and playing the same scenes again and again became pretty challenging.

An actor's job is to make the audience feel as though everything they're seeing is happening for the first and only time. Each scene must be infused with the intensity and passion it would have if the events were happening for real, right then. Audiences are smart. They can feel if someone is phoning it in. The show won't have the same electricity, and the people watching won't feel its emotional impact in the same visceral way. Six performances a week, year after year, song after song, gondola ride after gondola ride, keeping my energy and attention where they were supposed to be became my primary challenge.

Renew the Familiar

The challenge I faced onstage is the same challenge we all face in life: how to stay present and keep our mind focused on what we're doing while we're doing it. One of the tools I found most helpful in Christine-dom was one of constantly being on the lookout for something new. I could always bring my attention to a different instrument in the orchestra, for example, or a slightly different nuance in a line one of my fellow actors delivered. As long as I tuned the instrument of my attention, I also noticed new things—real or imaginary—in my onstage environment. They kept my sense of curiosity and excitement alive. Imagination, I discovered, is limitless.

There are certain times, of course, when no imagination is required, such as the night the famous chandelier did not crash on cue. The impeccable Hugh Panaro, who was playing the Phantom at the time, yelled, "Go!"—the cue for the crash—but nothing happened. I stood alongside my fellow actors, gazing upward, and the darn thing didn't budge. Mercifully, the wonderful John Cudia, as Raoul, ran out from the wings and whisked me away, as usual. We hoped the audience would decide we'd been spooked by the Phantom's holler. (Incidentally, they got the chandelier working again and crashed it after the curtain call at the end of the show—just so the audience could see its infamous descent right over their heads.)

One of the things that makes live theater so magical is knowing that it will never happen exactly the same way twice, realizing that what you see unfolding before your eyes is being created in real time, never to occur precisely that way again. Sometimes a technical glitch "helps" along this newness, as happened that night with the chandelier; more often, though, actors are the ones who have to keep the sparks flying.

This is important for the audience, of course, but it's also important for the actors and it's important for anyone seeking to uplevel their work. Why? Because autopilot is unfulfilling. Cultivating fresh eyes and ears, on the other hand, leads to innovation, creativity, problem solving, and staying actively engaged in what we're doing—which, in turn, helps us achieve new heights and breakthroughs.

Staying engaged from moment to moment doesn't help us only in our work lives, of course. When we practice being mindful of what we're doing while we're doing it, we awaken to the freshness that is ever present in our lives. This day we are living today will never happen again; the you who exists in this very moment will never be again. Even in the midst of repetition and monotony, whether we're standing in front of an audience or making our morning coffee alone in our kitchen, we can always find something fresh—and new. As Greek philosopher Heraclitus famously said, "No man ever steps in the same river twice, for it's not the same river and he is not the same man."

I was fascinated to learn about a study Yale University

professor Irwin Braverman conducted on his first-year medical students that involved cultivating fresh eyes. After noticing that the med students often missed details that would have clinched a diagnosis, Professor Braverman decided to use visual art in an effort to improve their "observational blindness." He formed a partnership with the Yale Center for British Art and required his students to take a fine-art class. The medical students in the study were asked to spend time looking at a classical painting. The study showed that after spending two hours examining the painting, the students were better able to diagnose patients. Training their brain to see the details actually helped them in their essential work. They even did a better job of identifying pertinent details than a second group who took an additional anatomy lecture, rather than the art class. Just as an actor's performance can improve when we actively make the effort to notice new details, those medical students' ability to make accurate diagnoses improved when they learned to look at things in a closer, more nuanced way.

When I actively practiced renewing the familiar on stage, I began to notice that I was also noticing new things off stage. Walking from the theater to my parking garage each night, I saw a seemingly endless array of delights: the colorful rows of flowers on display outside the deli on Eighth Avenue; a caramel-colored horse carrying one of New York's finest on his rounds through the city; dog walkers holding leashes by the fistful, effortlessly guiding five tail-wagging pooches at a time on their nightly walks. All of these sights had been there all along; it had just been a long time since I'd been able to see them. I had gotten so accustomed to my routine of hurrying home after every show that I had become blind to the abundance of beauty around me. The awareness I was developing to help keep the show fresh had an unexpected benefit in my personal life: the blinders were coming off, and I was seeing everything anew.

Find the Gift
A practice of cultivating fresh eyes

This is a daylong practice of intentionally looking at the world through fresh eyes. (Side effects may include being filled with love and gratitude.)

1. First thing in the morning, notice everything in your environment that someone else has given to you.

2. Throughout this one entire day, train your brain to find the gifts you've been given.

3. Repeat as often as you can.

Variation: For one full day, notice everything that's going right. Imagine if you woke up and got in the shower and found that the water wouldn't turn on. Then you went to get your morning coffee and the coffeepot had spilled all over the counter. You got in your car and the car wouldn't start. You would notice all of these things—so, instead, try noticing all of the things that *do* go your way. Whether it's technology that works or your timing being just right at important moments, there are sure to be many things that happen as you want them to in a day. Remember to take in the good as you move through this exercise.

Be Mindful

We perform our best at work and in life when we are as present as possible as often as possible. It's a matter of mindfulness, which meditation teacher Jon Kabat-Zinn defines as "awareness that arises through paying attention, on purpose, in the present moment, nonjudgmentally." Learning about mindfulness gave me a whole new understanding of what "stage presence" means. Have you ever noticed how magnetic someone is when they're really present and engaged with you? When you're talking to someone and you can feel that they are truly listening and giving you their undivided attention, it actually makes *them* compelling, doesn't it?

One of the most interesting studies I've ever encountered on mindfulness comes from Harvard professor Ellen Langer's research involving dolphin behavior. Tourists at Puerto Vallarta's Dolphin Adventure were given the Langer Mindfulness Scale to assess their level of mindfulness before they went swimming with the dolphins, and Langer and her colleagues found a fascinating correlation: the dolphins showed a preference for the more mindful group and spent the least time with the swimmers whose mindfulness scores were the lowest.

To further test their findings, Langer and her team ran a controlled experiment in which dolphin trainers were instructed to be mindful or mindless while swimming. The trainers in the mindful group were instructed to notice something new about the dolphins—some way in which they were different from the others or different than they had been the day before. The dolphins responded by staying with the mindful trainers longer, and by swimming faster and jumping higher for them.

I once took a wine tasting class that began with three grapes on a plate in front of each participant. We were instructed to eat the first grape and focus on the soft, juicy center, to really taste the fruit. For the second grape, we were invited to focus on the taste of the skin, to feel the texture of the tannins. For the third grape, we were asked to notice the tingle down the sides of our tongue, to feel for acidity. (Happily, we moved on soon thereafter to tasting several different varietals of wine.) I was amazed by how many different things there were to notice in one tiny piece of fruit. The exercise reminded me of Kabat-Zinn's mindfulness exercise, which uses a simple raisin.

Jon Kabat-Zinn's Raisin Consciousness Technique

A practice of bringing mindfulness to whatever we're doing to amplify our performance and keep things from becoming rote

1. Sit comfortably in a chair.

2. Place a raisin in your hand.

3. Examine the raisin as if you have never seen it before.

4. Imagine it as its "plump self" growing on the vine, surrounded by nature.

5. As you look at the raisin, become conscious of what you see: the shape, texture, color, size. Is it hard or soft?

6. Bring the raisin to your nose and smell it.

7. Are you anticipating eating the raisin? Is it difficult not to just pop it in your mouth?

8. How does the raisin feel? How small is it in your hand?

9. Place the raisin in your mouth. Become aware of what your tongue is doing.

10. Bite ever so lightly into the raisin. Feel its squishiness.

11. Chew three times and then stop.

12. Describe the flavor of the raisin. What is the texture?

As you make your way through each step of this exercise, you'll find that it's like you're seeing, feeling, smelling, and tasting the raisin for the first time. Now that you know how to do this, bring the same awareness and attention to other things in your life!

Give Yourself a Break

Athletes, musicians, and actors will all tell you, the more demanding the performance, the greater the need for personal renewal. To perform at a high level over a long period of time requires an unwavering commitment to radical self-care. As Meredith Zara, my college voice teacher always said, "A tired body means a tired voice." And I'll never forget what another performance coach said to me when I was in a frenzy of adrenal overload: "Your only job in all the world is to relax."

Sometimes we need to push ourselves to climb higher, yes. But what many of us—especially those of us who are Type A workaholics or insecure overachievers—need is to get off our own backs. We need to give ourselves permission to slow down, to bring a sense of ease to what we're doing, or maybe even to stop for a time. Taking the occasional break isn't weakness; it's part of what it takes to be our best over the long haul. We can't keep our eyes fresh when we're so tired we can barely keep them open.

On January 9, 2006, *Phantom* broke the record, formerly held by *Cats*, for longest-running Broadway show of all time. The supervisors and creative team wanted the show that night to be at its absolute best. New costumes were built to replace any that looked the slightest bit weathered. A new photo shoot was done, and the photos outside the theater were updated. New souvenir programs were printed. The set got a fresh coat of paint, new props were made—everything sparkled as I imagined it did when the show first opened, back in 1988.

The supervisors wanted the cast to be at their best that night as well. A couple of months beforehand, they came to me and asked, "What can we do to help you? Would you like additional time off?"

At first, I felt hesitant to take them up on their offer. Theater actors generally get only two weeks of vacation time per year, and I had already used up mine. I didn't want to show any signs of weakness. The first year I'd played Christine, I hadn't taken any time off; I'd performed six nights a week that entire year without taking a vacation, partly because I was so happy to be playing the part and partly because I wanted so badly to prove myself. By the record-breaking show, I had also become a record breaker as *Phantom*'s longest-running female star. Still, the desire to prove my worth ran deep.

In the end, I accepted their offer, and a few weeks before the record-breaking show, I did something that seemed completely indulgent and self-serving: I went to a spa. For a week. By myself. And . . . *ahh*. My shoulders dropped down from their usual position at my earlobes. I'd been in desperate need of a break for a while, but I was so concerned with what other people would think that I almost hadn't accepted the offer of extra time off. I was always hyper vigilant about staving off any perception that I was being a baby, that I was weak—or, worst of all, that I'd become a diva. But stepping away from *Phantom*-land for a while was the best thing I could have done. The show was in the hands of some very capable actresses, the Christine understudies, while I was gone, and thanks to my getaway, I was rested and ready when the record-breaking night arrived.[6]

---

6. *Those fire escape stairs never looked so good as they did that night, when practically everyone who'd ever played Christine was in the audience—along with Andrew Lloyd Webber, Cameron Mackintosh, Hal Prince, and the entire creative team. I knew my nervousness would cause my mouth to go dry, so I took a pill that creates saliva. It worked a little too well. Throughout the show, I had to fight not to drool all over the stage.*

I'm sad to say that I am not even close to being alone when it comes to having concerns regarding taking time off work. According to a 2017 study conducted by the Harris Poll, the average US employee who receives paid vacation has taken only slightly more than half—54 percent—of the days allotted them in the past twelve months. Furthermore, even when they do take vacations, two out of three people surveyed said they do at least some work on their personal time off.

Why do we do this? Mostly out of fear, the Harris Poll's findings suggest. Three of the most common reasons people cited for not taking their vacation days were getting behind on their work (34 percent), believing no one else at their company could do the work while they were out (30 percent), and feeling like they should never be disconnected (21 percent). In other words, it's frequently not our dedication to our work but our fear and insecurity that keeps us chained to our work environments.

The irony is that so many of us refuse to take time off because we're afraid our work won't get done, and yet the research is clear that using vacation days actually makes us more productive—and even more likely to increase our income. A study released in July 2016, for example, found that people who took fewer than ten of their vacation days per year had only a 34.6 percent likelihood of receiving a raise or bonus in a three-year period of time, while people who took more than ten of their vacation days had an impressive 65.4 percent chance of receiving a raise or bonus.

It's not just the big breaks that are important, either; taking little breaks is effective, too. In the book *The Power of Full Engagement*, authors Jim Loehr and Tony Schwartz talk about "ultradian rhythms"—90- to 120-minute cycles of wakefulness and sleepiness that are repeated throughout a 24-hour day. These biological rhythms, say Loehr and Schwartz, "help to account for the ebb and flow of our energy throughout the day. Physiological measures such as heart rate, hormonal levels, muscle tension, and brain-wave activity all increase during the first part of the cycle—and so does alertness. After an hour or so, these measures start to decline. Somewhere between 90 and 120 minutes, the body begins to crave a period of rest and recovery."

Applying this to everyday life, Loehr and Schwartz suggest dividing your workday into 90-minute segments, with 15- to 20-minute breaks in between each one. This allows your body time to rest and renew itself—which means that when you return to work, you have the energy and focus you need to complete whatever tasks are at hand. (This isn't just applicable in an office environment, either: What happens ninety minutes into *Phantom*? Intermission!)

Take Time to Play

"What do you do for play?" my therapist asked during our first session.

I was silent for a long time as I scoured the recesses of my mind. "Um . . . does sleeping count?" I finally asked.

It did not.

For a long time, I thought, as many of us do, that the harder you work, the better you perform. My therapist helped me see that continual high performance without playtime is simply not sustainable. All animals play, and we human animals need to as well.

Stuart Brown, coauthor of *Play: How It Shapes the Brain, Opens the Imagination, and Invigorates the Soul*, defines play as "an ancient, voluntary, inherently plea-surable, apparently purposeless activity or process that is undertaken for its own sake, and that strengthens our muscles and our social skills, fertilizes brain activity, tempers and deepens our emotions, takes us out of time, and enables a state of balance and poise." More simply put, play is something you do for fun that makes you feel good. I hope this kind of activity is already a part of your vacations, but spending only two weeks per year (or less, if you're like most of those people from the Harris Poll!) engaged in some form of play is not enough. It's so essential to your well-being to find something that is authentically enjoyable for you—something you find nourishing, soothing, relaxing—and incorporate it into your life on a regular basis.

One of my favorite playtime activities is walking outdoors and seeing the beauty in nature, so I was delighted when Dr. Chad Larson, a San Diego naturopath, told me that doing so actually has scientifically proven health benefits. Studies were conducted on a Japanese practice called *shinrin-yoku,* or "forest bathing." The practice is simple: leisurely walks in nature during which a person slows down and tunes in to the smells, textures, tastes, and sights around them. Field experiments in twenty-four forests across Japan showed that forest bathing promotes healthful physiological changes in individuals, including healthier stress-hormone levels and lower pulse rates, blood pressure, and sympathetic nerve activity—benefits that we simply do not get when we stay indoors.

Many of us recognize that spending time in nature makes us feel good, but now science is teaching us the reasons why.

The Danish culture offers another way of relaxing that is beginning to catch on in the United States: *hygge* (pronounced "*hue*-gah"). This word often translates to "coziness," but it can also be described as "dwelling poetically." *Hygge* is about creating peaceful, calm, pleasurable experiences or environments, either alone or with family and friends. *Hygge* is not another thing to do; it has no agenda. It can be as simple as enjoying a hot cup of tea on a cold, rainy day or lighting a candle and snuggling up under a soft blanket. My mom creates *hygge* for me whenever I come to visit. She preheats an electric throw for me to curl up in and makes sure I have freshly washed, soft pajamas and fluffy socks to put on. The genius of *hygge* is that it can be practically anything that makes you feel good. It's the most gentle kind of play there is, and it's something you can do for yourself or someone you love at virtually any moment in your day.

Staying true to a strong work ethic does not mean working yourself weary and never taking a break; in fact, it's just the contrary. It's only when we take time to play and relax and, whenever possible, bring a spirit of playfulness and ease to our work that we truly excel. Our inner life influences everything we do, and being present takes energy. When we aren't filling our own cup, we can't give our best.

> For those who prefer indoor playtime, Happify.com is a great resource. There you will find computer games designed to increase positive emotions. In my favorite game on the site, you begin by writing negative words on animated balloons— and then you get to pop them with a slingshot that fires away each time you click your mouse. It's simple, easy, and unexpectedly gratifying!

Embrace Uncertainty

Even in a well-oiled machine like *Phantom*, anything can happen at any time. Playing the same scenes night after night, hundreds of times, didn't completely alleviate the sense of unpredictability, because nothing is guaranteed when you're live. Learning to maneuver within the ever-present uncertainty was wonderful training for life both on and off the stage.

Live performance requires that we continually adjust to how things are, rather than how we would like them to be. The extreme version of this is improvisational theater, where actors have to invent plot, characters, and dialogue on the fly. In her beautiful book *Improv Wisdom*, Stanford University professor emerita Patricia Ryan Madson writes that we can learn much from this approach: "As we come to accept insecurity as the norm, as our home ground, it becomes familiar and less frightening. Sometimes this sense of being off-balance is exhilarating and reminds us of the impermanence and fragility of life, nudging us to appreciate each imperfect, teetering moment we are alive. Perhaps, like surfers, we can come to feel the power of the waves, the majesty of the elements, and a sense of our own place in this swirling universe." *Phantom* is clearly not improvisational theater, but we still had to be surfers sometimes. The chandelier malfunction I mentioned earlier was one of those times. Another was a different technical difficulty—this one with the gondola.

Before I was in *Phantom*, I assumed tracks on the floor were what allowed the gondola to glide along the stage so magically during the scene "The Journey." In fact, the mechanism that moves the boat is even more magical than I thought. There are no tracks along the floor. The gondola is on wheels, and it runs on an infrared system—just like a remote-controlled toy car. There is a stagehand in the wings, just off stage left, controlling its movement with a joystick. When all goes well, the gondola travels across a huge portion of the stage and makes a large figure eight before stopping in its resting position slightly upstage center.

One night, just as "The Journey" was beginning, the gondola jerked and then stopped. I glanced into the wings out of the corner of my eye. Fred, who was manning the joystick, was clearly having no luck getting things rolling again. We were what felt like miles away from where we were supposed to be—and we had a whole song to finish. We couldn't stay in our faraway position in the broken-down boat. So, what did we do? We improvised! Howard McGillin, who was playing the Phantom that night, was smooth enough to simply step out of the gondola and reach for my hand. Without a second thought, I stepped out with him, and the two of us walked on water for the rest of the scene. Crisis averted!

Not all professions demand the kind of moment-to-moment adaptability acting does, of course. If you think about your own profession, however, you'll probably find that at least some aspect of your job requires a degree of flexibility and willingness to roll with change. And even if your job doesn't, your personal life certainly does. Life, after all, is one big bundle of unknowns, a never-ending sea of change, whether we like it or not.

When we can find ease within uncertainty, we cultivate an empowering sense of agency and self-trust. As Pema Chödrön writes in her book *Comfortable with Uncertainty*, "This moving away from comfort and security, this stepping out into what is unknown and uncharted, and shaky—that's called liberation."

Life is not fixed, and we are not meant to be steady and stable all the time. With practice, though, we can become better surfers who are able to keep our balance when the big waves come. So savor the nuances, immerse yourself in the amorphous details, treat yourself like a prima donna diva, relax, see art, get outside, find what's new—and, for heaven's sake, take a play break. This day, this moment, won't ever happen again—and that's a beautiful thing.

Questions to Live By

- How can you bring fresh eyes and ears to your work? How about your personal life?

- Can you imagine approaching your work with a sense of playfulness and ease?

- What do you do for play?

- Do you allow yourself to take breaks when you need them?

- How often do you say "yes" to whatever's happening in the moment?

Chapter 8:

Adjust Your Perspective

A hundred times a day I remind myself that
my inner and outer life depends on the labors
of other men, living and dead, and that I must
exert myself in order to give in the measure as I
have received and am still receiving.

—Albert Einstein

"I'm losing steam," I confessed to my friend Scott on the phone. There was no point trying to pretend everything was fine. Our friendship spanned almost twenty years; he could always tell when something was off with me. "I just don't know if I can do this anymore."

I was in my eighth year of playing Christine six nights a week, and I was really feeling the strain. This wasn't just me being overdramatic with a close friend; I honestly wasn't sure I could keep going. A toll collector at the Lincoln Tunnel had asked if I was okay the day prior, and only then had I realized I'd been crying during my drive to work—an almost Pavlovian response that regularly occurred as I crossed the threshold from New Jersey to NYC each night. The closer I got to the theater, the more anxious I became that I would not be capable of delivering the kind of performance Broadway requires.

"I'm so worn out," I confessed to Scott. "I feel guilty saying it out loud. I know how many people would trade places with me in a second. I totally get how fortunate I am to be where I am, but I've been practicing everything I know how to do and I'm just spent."

Scott listened to my lamentations and consoled me without judgment. Before we hung up, he was quiet for a long moment. Then he said, in the understanding tone of a friend who knows exactly what you need, "Let's meet for coffee next week."

One week later, I sat down across from him in Bunbury's Café in Piermont, New York, coffee in hand. Without a word, he handed me a box. It was purple, and he had stenciled the word "Perspective" on top of it.

"Open it," he encouraged me.

I lifted the lid. Inside, I found clippings he had scoured the Internet to find, from people all over the world talking about how seeing *Phantom* had impacted them. Some of them mentioned me by name. I sat there, tears rolling down my cheeks and into my cappuccino, as I read account after account. One woman wrote about how she had seen *Phantom* with her mother before she passed away, and how it was a memory she would always cherish. A man said he had saved up for a year to take his family on a trip to New York to see the show, and that he would always remember the look in his daughter's eyes as he watched her watch it. There were several notes from young women who'd had the same moment seeing *Phantom* that I'd had so long ago when I saw *Annie* for the first time.

I had always felt honored to be a part of the show, but that Perspective box refocused me on the impact one night in the theater could make. Despite the fact that I was really struggling with burnout, sometimes a sense of quiet joy would overtake me, rather in spite of myself. In those moments when I thought about the clippings my friend had collected for me, those 1,500 audience members sitting out there in the dark were no longer strangers; they were individuals in whose lives I had the potential to create a lasting memory. It shifted my attention from "How am I going to get through my 927th performance?" to "Who is that one person out there who is going to see this show for the very first and perhaps only time?" I was reminded of what a privilege it was to be able to take someone on a journey for those two and half hours. That shift in perspective didn't make my exhaustion disappear, but it did often help fill my gas tank when I was running on fumes. Because of Scott and his incredible gift, I discovered that a sense of purpose is the most powerful motivator on earth.

Value Your Role

In the midst of our day-to-day activities, it can be easy to forget that what we do and how we do it makes a difference. We can get so caught up in the minutiae of our responsibilities that it can be easy to lose sight of what really matters— why it's so important to dig deep and do whatever it is we do to the best of our ability. Often, we feel we aren't doing enough. We think only big, world-changing endeavors matter. I was certainly guilty of this during my time in *Phantom*: I sometimes found myself doubting that this career choice of mine was a meaningful enough one on a planet so in need of healing.

Oprah often tells the story of when she told her friend and mentor Maya Angelou that her work building schools in Africa would be her legacy, and Maya schooled her by telling her, "Your legacy is every life you touch." My dad imparted a similar lesson to me throughout my life. As a young performer, I remember tearfully confessing to him that I was afraid pursuing a career in musical theater was selfish. The idea of doing something I found so inherently enjoyable for a living made me feel guilty. *People are digging ditches and building shelters for the homeless,* I thought, *and what am I doing? I'm singing show tunes.* My dad was the first to help me understand the profoundly valuable role art of all kinds plays in our lives. He began recording the annual Kennedy Center Honors on TV and mailing me the VHS tapes. One of our favorites was the year Broadway legend Julie Harris was honored. I later read that when asked what she would do if the world were going to end the following day, she answered, "I would go to the theater." The late, great Ms. Harris also said, "What is thrilling about the theater is that it's a forum where people come and for those two or three hours belong to something, to ideas, to a feeling of being a member of the human race . . . I want to touch people with the meaning of life."

Think about all the manners in which you touch people each day, even in small ways—the neighbors you wave to from your driveway, the cashier who rings you up at the grocery store, the coworkers you exchange emails with or stop to chat with in the hall. On any given day, we all have countless chances to touch another person—and, as Maya Angelou told Oprah, it isn't just the big things that matter. Our legacy is every single life we touch. A 2003 *New Yorker* article called "Jumpers," about people who have jumped from the Golden Gate Bridge, offers a heartbreaking example of this concept: Dr. Jerome Motto, a Bay Area psychiatrist, lost more than one patient to suicide by bridge, but the one that affected him most involved a short, poignant note: "I'm going to walk to the bridge," it read. "If one person smiles at me on the way, I will not jump."

How we show up in our daily lives, and the quality of our attention, matters. Even a smile we offer to a stranger on the street could make a difference we can never imagine. It helps to remind ourselves of this truth on a regular basis, though, because it's an easy one to forget when all the thousands of details of life begin to muddy up our view. And that's where perspective shifts can help us. I was delighted to discover that the word "perspective" comes from the same Latin root as the word "spectacles." Makes sense, doesn't it? Perspective adjusts our vision; it helps us to see clearly. And seeing clearly is the first step to leaving a beautiful legacy in this world, one small act at a time.

The Perspective Box

A practice of adjusting your vision to help yourself gain perspective when you need it most

Create a Perspective Box—for yourself or someone else, either a physical one or a virtual one, perhaps in the form of a file on your computer.

What to put in it:

- An "achievements" list: What have you accomplished in your life thus far? What big achievements can you lay claim to? What about the small ones?
- An "obstacles overcome" list: What difficulties have you surmounted in your life? What challenges have you faced? (Acknowledge how hard you've tried. Effort matters more than results.)
- Thank-you notes you've received (also make a note of verbal thanks, handshakes, pats on the back, et cetera)
- Your mission statement: What are your most important reasons for doing what you're doing?

(continued on next page)

Going forward: At the end of each day, write down either: 1) three ways your efforts today made a difference or will make a difference to another person or group of people; 2) three things you did well today; or 3) three times you felt loved, acknowledged, or included today. Put it all in your Perspective Box.[7]

Consider the Ripple Effect

Not one stage actor I know went into the business because they hoped to strike it rich. Far too many, however, pursued performance in hopes of fulfilling an inner need that wasn't met in childhood. In recent years, I've had time to reflect on my *Phantom* journey and examine my own reasons for feeling it was so important to work my way to the top—a question I never paused long enough to ponder in my twenties. I loved performing, to be sure, but there was something more driving me—a need that I thought only "making it" could fulfill. I was far less concerned with the *why* of my path than I was with the *what* and the *how* back then.

Now I understand the reason author Simon Sinek is encouraging leaders to "start with why." To stay inspired to do our best work, to actually be fulfilled by what we're doing, we need to have a deep sense of purpose. This is the gift of perspective: it shines a spotlight on the purpose behind our endeavors.

A number of studies have shown how important it is to find our work meaningful. In a study published in 2010, for example, Brent D. Rosso, PhD, and his colleagues found

---

7. *I've been very moved by how people have taken this idea and run with it. I was invited to give a keynote presentation for the fiftieth-anniversary gala of a charitable organization. On each table, the centerpiece was a purple Perspective Box containing clippings and photos highlighting the people and organizations that charity had helped over the past fifty years. At another event, the CEO received a purple Perspective Box as a retirement gift; it held clippings from colleagues about the impact he had made on the lives of everyone within the organization.*

that people who believe their work has meaning display increased motivation, engagement, empowerment, career development, job satisfaction, individual performance and personal fulfillment, and lower stress levels. Meanwhile, Amy Wrzesniewski, a professor of organizational behavior at Yale who has conducted a wealth of research on the experience of work as a job, career, or calling, insists that "job crafting"—changing the way you think about and execute your job in order to turn it into something you love—is vital to job satisfaction and individual well-being. Yet another study found that when people doing stressful fund-raising jobs kept a journal for a few days about how their work made a difference, they increased their hourly effort by 29 percent.

Think about your own job for a moment. Whatever it is that you do, there is no doubt that it has value beyond what is obviously visible in your day-to-day routine. Perhaps you're a landscape architect and someone who has recently suffered a great loss walked through one of the outdoor spaces you designed today and found their first moment of peace and comfort in the beauty of their surroundings. Maybe you work for a foundation that offers scholarships to underserved communities and, because of a phone call or email you sent today, one more young person will be able to break a long cycle of poverty in their family and start building a better future. Perhaps you're a receptionist and your smile was a bright spot in fifty people's day today. I know you might not always see how what you're doing matters, but if you really stop to think about the ripple effect of your daily efforts and how they are impacting individual lives—or will impact them in the future—you'll find there isn't a box big enough to hold all that perspective.

Help Others, Help Yourself

"There are two kinds of people in life," says author and communication expert Leil Lowndes. "Those who walk into a room and say, 'Well, here I am!' and those who walk in and say, 'Ahh, there you are.' Be the second type of person."

One way to practice being that second type of person is by continually adjusting our perspective. We get to choose how we approach every activity we engage in, and the quality of presence we bring to each. Richard J. Davidson, PhD, the *New York Times* best-selling coauthor of *The Emotional Life of Your Brain*, explains this idea in an interview with 1440 Multiversity: "When we run or play tennis, we don't normally invoke the explicit intention that we're doing it primarily for the benefit of others. But we could, and that may change the nature of those kinds of activities in important ways. As a practitioner as well as a scientist, I have a lot of reason to believe that when we do things with an altruistic intention it produces different kinds of effects, including biological effects. I invite people to try it—engage in your activities of leisure with altruistic intention—and see what happens."

Acting selflessly, then, can actually make us happier. According to a study published in 2014 by Yale's Wrzesniewski, along with Barry Schwartz of Swarthmore College and a number of other scholars, it can also lead to greater material success. After conducting research on more than ten thousand West Point cadets over the course of ten years, Wrzesniewski, Schwartz, and their colleagues found that those cadets who came to the academy with mainly "instrumental" motives in mind (e.g., in hopes of elevating their future careers) experienced far less professional success down the line than those who had come to the school with mainly "internal" motives (e.g., a desire to serve their country). Even those who had some internal motives mixed in with their instrumental motives did not achieve the same level of success as those with purely internal motives. In other words, the cadets with selfless motives actually got furthest ahead in life.

Framed the right way, any job, any action, can be about serving other people—even when you're the one standing in the spotlight. The job of an actor, for example, can be to garner praise and applause for himself or to serve the writer's intention to tell the story and take the audience on an emotional journey. Giving your best, standing in your power, sharing what is yours to share—these things can be done from a place of needy narcissism or from a stance of selfless service. We get to decide which.

I learned this lesson quickly when I began my run in *Phantom*. In my early days of playing Christine, as I began to explore my own depths, I made the mistake of overindulging my own emotion in the show, for my own catharsis. This happened mostly in a scene in Act Two where Christine goes to visit her late father's grave and sings the heart-rending song "Wishing You Were Somehow Here Again." It was always an easy scene for me to connect with emotionally because of my close relationship with my own father: all I had to do to create the right emotional connection to sing "Wishing" was to feel into what it would be like if I were standing beside my own father's grave.

It's important to lean into your own emotional truth as an actor, but doing so requires a delicate balance. I soon discovered that when I overindulged, I was making it about me. Some internal part of me was taking pride in my ability to open a vein onstage (*Look how emotionally invested I can be! Look how I can gush tears!*). A more audience-centric performance meant keeping my heart open enough that the audience could feel their own hearts, think about their own lost loved ones, experience the story within the landscape of their own emotional truth, but not to be so overwhelmed by my emotions that the audience became concerned about me, the actress, and whether or not I'd make it to the end of the song.

"Why reach for something you can never fully attain?" asks Daniel H. Pink, author of multiple best-selling books on human behavior. "But it's also a source of allure. The joy is in the pursuit more than the realization. In the end, mastery attracts precisely because mastery eludes." Yes, mastery certainly does elude. It's not possible to be altruistic 100 percent of the day any more than it's possible to perform a perfect ten every night. But pushing ourselves toward our highest and best can be exhilarating and enlivening. So why not give *giving* all we've got? When we fall short, which we inevitably will, we can take comfort in this humbling advice from the Buddhists: "Act always as if the future of the universe depended on what you did, while laughing at yourself for thinking that whatever you do makes any difference."

Keeping our eyes focused on the unselfish impact of all our endeavors is actually the most selfish thing we can do, because it will benefit us just as much as—if not more than—the people we seek to serve. And, honestly, we'll have more fun doing it; it's far more fulfilling to reach deeply into our reserves and give something our all for the benefit of others, than it is to be self-serving. It's something we can practice—every day, with everything we do. We can think about who we're helping, letting our good hearts motivate us toward our best actions. In doing so, we may just change someone's life for the better—including our own.

Questions to Live By

- What is the difference you make in your work or professional life right now?

- What motivates you to give your all, even when you're tired and you've been at it for a long time?

- How can you stay motivated in the coming weeks, months, years?

- What did you do today that benefited someone else?

- In whose life have you made the biggest difference?

- How can you adjust your view and stay focused on the value of the role you play?

Chapter 9:

Remember Your Curtain Call

Sometimes from sorrow, for no reason, you sing.
—William Stafford

A ll things end. I was overflowing with gratitude as I walked toward the Majestic Theatre on April 15, 2006. My only goal for my final show was to be fully present—to inhabit every single moment in its entirety. I wanted to carry the memory of the whole experience with me, wherever life might take me next.

I walked through the alley and stopped at the red stage door as I had a thousand times before. Gripping the door-knob, I took a deep breath. Already the corners of my eyes were filling. Wally, the stage doorman, hugged me before handing me the dressing room key, marked "Daaé." I initialed the box next to my name on the callboard and stuck a pushpin into the note I'd written for the cast and crew. It was a quote from Dr. Seuss: "Don't cry because it's over;

smile because it happened." My note said that I'd be smiling all evening.

Outside my dressing room were cards and gifts from castmates who'd arrived before me. A steady stream of well-wishers came to visit right up until curtain time. Craig, our teddy bear of a stage manager, hugged me for a long time. As he left my dressing room, Howard McGillin entered. Howard and I had worked together for more performances than I could count. We had become the longest-running leads of all time in *Phantom*. A wonderful actor, a Broadway legend, and a phenomenal human being, Howard knew how much this final evening meant to me, and he came to see me armed with hugs, gifts, and—best of all—the understanding gaze of someone who'd played a role for a very long time. He squeezed my hands and gave me a meaningful nod before heading back across the hall to his dressing room.

As the music began to play through the monitor—my cue for a decade to leave the dressing room and head to the stage—I took a long look in the full-length mirror. I would never again put on this costume or wig. The chandelier was rising over the audience.

When I made my first entrance, I felt the love of my costars beaming around me like a halo. The entire cast is onstage for Christine's first aria; when it was time for me to sing, I heard sniffling. The actress who played Meg handed me the scarf with tears in her eyes, and when I glanced to my right at Madame Giry, she was biting a quivering lip. David Lai, our beloved maestro, looked up at me with even more love and support in his eyes than he had given me during the 1,300-something performances we'd done together.

The music started and I tried to sing, but what came out was more of a heartfelt whisper:

Think of me, think of me fondly
When we've said good-bye
Remember me, every so often
Promise me you'll try . . .

What a gift I'd been handed—such an incredible role in a beloved piece of musical theater. With each costume change, I willed myself to remember what it felt like to wear such works of art. What a privilege it had been, despite the challenging aspects—what a joyride. The night was even more emotional than I'd expected. It was over in the blink of a very bloodshot eye.

As I made my last walk down the center of the stage for my final bow, the rows of cast members on either side of me each threw a single, long-stemmed red rose toward my feet to line my path. Howard, the Phantom, came down after me and handed me a bouquet. After the final company bow, he quieted the audience and gave a curtain speech, telling the patrons that tonight was the final show for me, Broadway's longest-running female star. The cast and audience applauded. And the curtain closed.

It was an indescribably special night, made even more special by the email I found in my inbox when I got home that evening. It was from my dad—typed, as always, with one finger—and it recapped my entire journey from my parents' perspective. "What more could a parent hope for than to see a child reach a goal in life and be there to live it with her," he wrote. "Keep on flying, child, and carry me on your wings. It's been a wonderful ride. You and *Phantom* have given us so many memories to savor in the coming years."

But those years my dad looked forward to turned out to be fewer than either of us expected.

Only a year and a half had passed since I'd left *Phantom*. It was a snowy Michigan morning on December 16, 2007, a perfect day for comfort food. So when my dad woke up, he put on a pot roast for that night's dinner. He and my mom, both in their mid-sixties, looked out the window and joked about making snow angels. Then Dad sat in his favorite recliner to watch *CBS Sunday Morning* and started having chest pains. The ambulance came quickly enough, but by the time the cardiologist met my mom and sister in the hospital, Dad was gone.

Dive All The Way In

We are often advised to "lean into" our difficult feelings. What I did when my father died, quite involuntarily, was not so much to lean into my feelings as to, with palms clasped arrow-like over my head, plummet off a high dive into a seemingly endless ocean of anguish. My grief was like a black, bottomless liquid in which I choked and snorted and gasped for each tiny hiccup of air. Hal Prince always described the Phantom when he is first unmasked as "mewling and puking" as he writhes on his knees across the stage. Those words from Shakespeare's *As You Like It* were a fitting description of me each night at 4:00 a.m. as I keened on the bathroom floor.

I tried to rally, told myself it was time to begin climbing out of the hole I was in. I'd known depression before, and I feared that this time, I might stay in that dark place forever. And then, one night in bed, when I had nothing else to help me sleep, I picked up the copy of *The Prophet* my cousin had given me at my dad's funeral. Unbeknownst to her, my dad loved the book and had recommended it to me, but I'd never gotten around to reading it. I flipped it open to a random page.

"Some of you say, 'Joy is greater than sorrow,' and others say, 'Nay, sorrow is the greater,'" I read. "But I say unto you they are inseparable. The deeper that sorrow carves into your being, the more joy you can contain. . . .

Your joy is your sorrow unmasked." I gasped. I'd been letting my grief have its full way with me. I'd been feeling
like a scab had been ripped off of my entire body. I'd been
walking around with my insides on the outside. My sorrow
had unmasked me completely. And, realizing this, I felt my
anguish give way—just for a moment—as if it had slipped
down a rabbit hole, quite in spite of me, into a realm of
such deep compassion and such profound okayness that I
felt as though I were being carried. I sensed a visceral kin-
ship with everyone who had ever lost a person whose very
presence had made them feel whole.

The great gift that suffering leaves in its wake is that
when we are raw we are also more open—to love, to beauty,
to compassion, and to our connection with all that is. As
Jan Frazier writes, "A breaking heart feels exquisitely alive,
even while the pain might be breathtaking." Within this
aliveness, we lose our false sense of separation, the protective layer we sometimes walk around with in our day-to-day
lives. We feel the fullness of sorrow, but we are also open
enough to experience a felt sense of the oneness of all things.
My father's death was the single most heartbreaking experience of my life—but it was also an awakening.

Be Here, Not There

Sages throughout history have assured us that what we
seek is not "out there" but always right here, where we
stand. This truth is often difficult to recognize, but sometimes something triggers a reflex that causes us to gaze
down at our feet—and in that moment we realize we've
been standing all along on the portal to peace. I tasted
that other realm after my father died, just as I tasted it as a
four-year-old while coloring on my porch in Detroit. And I
tasted it once more, in 2007 . . .

On a Friday, I had a CT scan for what turned out to be

a harmless cyst in my neck. The test showed an unexpected abnormality, however—partial paralysis of my tongue—so, on Monday, I was sent for an MRI of my head. I had noticed that lately certain words requiring major use of the tongue (like "Google") had sometimes been tricky to artic-ulate, but I hadn't thought much of it.

There are twelve cranial nerves in your head, each charged with a different duty. The MRI showed a small tumor at the entry point of my brain, pressing on cranial nerve number twelve—the nerve that controls the motor function on the left side of the tongue.

I went to Boston to see Dr. Zeitels, one of the leading voice specialists in the world, and he was not subtle. "If you treat the thing," he said, "you'll have a speech imped-iment for the rest of your life and *you'll never sing again.*"

My case was taken before the tumor review board at Mt. Sinai Hospital in New York. I would have to wait two weeks before finding out if my ability to sing would soon be taken away forever.

As anyone who has had to wait for medical test results will understand all too well, those two weeks felt like two years. I had far too much time to think. Yes, I ruminated over worst-case scenarios—but some of my thoughts surprised me. I thought of how often I had taken my ability to sing for granted. I thought of how critical I'd been of my voice when a tone didn't measure up to my impossibly high standards. I thought of how often I'd lamented the shortcomings of my abilities and how seldom I'd celebrated them. And even though no one ever said that the tumor in my head was life-threat-ening, I thought about my own mortality. I felt the fragility of everything. And it created an urgency I wasn't expecting.

Before this experience, I would have expected that I would want to run out and record an album or star in another Broadway show if someone told me that my ability to sing might be taken away forever. But I didn't—not in the least. In fact, the idea of finding another role to play didn't even cross my mind. The urgency I felt was about only one thing: how to fully inhabit the role of *being me*.

Drop the Rope

I think many of us, when we're young, look forward to our older, wiser years. We imagine an idealized image of the person we'll be then, when we'll finally become our capital-"S" Self—the most grounded, authentic, and powerful "Self" of our highest potential. We think one day, with enough effort and the right tools, we will become someone who shows up, fully present, for all the people we encounter; someone who gives indiscriminately the gifts we have to offer to the world; someone who takes direction from within without fretting over what other people on the outside might think. We take for granted that we'll have time to grow ourselves into that better Self in our later years—or at least I did. But my tumor diagnosis and the sudden loss of my father reminded me of an unequivocal truth: To grow into an elderly person is not a given. It is a privilege, a luxury, one to yearn for as a six-year-old yearns for Christmas.

But if living well into old age isn't guaranteed, we might wonder, how can we become our older, wiser, more centered Selves *now*? How can we cut to the front of the line of Buddhahood?

Maybe we're asking the wrong questions. Maybe trying to hurry up and become a new, improved version of ourselves so we can finally deem ourselves acceptable is a fruitless pursuit. Many of us have been searching for years under every rock to find the one key that will unlock the door marked ENLIGHTENMENT, but for all our years of seeking, for all the books we've read and workshops and retreats we've attended, for all the teachers and gurus to whom we've paid countless sums in order to lift ourselves up, something always pulls us back down like Ophelia's skirts and lands us in the muck again. Maybe what we need, then, is to stop striving for betterment and try an entirely new approach.

For me, experiencing the felt sense of my own impermanence caused a new pathway to present itself. I'd been pulling with all my might for years—left, right, left, right—in an endless tug-of-war between The Me I Think I Should Be (practically perfect in every way) and The Me I See Who's Not Enough (a broken self relentlessly in need of repair). But, through no wisdom on my part, one day, rather in spite of myself, a solution to my tug-of-war whispered from someplace deep within:

> *Drop.*
> *The.*
> *Rope.*

A surge of peace accompanied this new thought. *What if this is as good as I ever get? What if I stop believing I should be anything other than exactly who I am? What if who I am right now—without my starring role, without my beloved father, even potentially without my ability to sing—is actually good enough?* These questions brought forth a profound recognition: I had compassion for the being that was still there underneath. I could live with her. I could accept her. I could even actually love her.

When I allowed myself to accept this possibility—that I could be enough even without any further self-improvement, even without the "talent" that made me "special"—it felt like I was setting down a box of bricks I didn't know I'd been carrying. Authentic presence, emptying out and letting go, took on a whole new meaning. I'd struggled for so long as a person and as a performer—overworking, trying to be better, believing I had to be the best. Inhabiting our field of power is about more than how we show up in the world outside us. It's about how we relate to the being within us. What it really means is that we are able to stand out in the open, trusting in our own inherent worth, knowing that we are enough exactly as we are—in all of our flawed humanity.

When my cell phone finally rang with the decision from the tumor review board, I took a deep breath—and let it out as the voice on the other end of the line gave me my life back. The doctors and surgeons had agreed that because I used my voice for a living, a conservative "watch and wait" approach would be acceptable. No surgery. No radiation. Nothing.

I'm happy to report that the little tumor on my brain stem has held steady for more than a decade now and is expected to remain dormant. I am enormously grateful to be able to continue to sing. But I'm also grateful for what I learned by walking through that fearful experience: I was never my voice. Since then, I've had a new respect for Rilke's words: "When all I wanted was to sing, I was accorded the honor of living."

Drop the Rope

A practice of experiencing the witnessing presence that holds all aspects of your self

1. Hold out your hands, palms facing the sky.

2. Imagine in your left hand the "you" who strives for improvement, the taskmaster who insists you should be the perfect size, the best at everything you do, and so on.

3. Imagine in your right hand the "you" who insists you'll never get it right, the one who tells you you'll never be good enough, you shouldn't even try, and so on.

4. "See" the inner taskmaster in the left hand and the inner flagellator in the right.

(continued on next page)

5. Now, as you gaze back and forth at these two opposing sides, ask yourself, "Who is the one doing the holding?" Can the observing presence—the larger you who is witnessing both aspects—love both extremes? Can you drop the rope in the tug-of-war and be the loving presence that holds it all?

Rewrite the Script

To live an unmasked life is to sense our place within the vast living universe, to meet experience with a wide-open heart, to dive into the molten center of pain and stumble out the other side—wounded but still walking, and more connected to humanity for the journey. That deep connection—the sense of no separate "me" or "you"—is the essence of the unmasked place. It's where the bitterness of loss and the sweetness of love meet. When we're in that place, even the idea of a "self" feels like a mask.

We need not wait for a sudden loss or a scary diagnosis to wake us up, though. Staying mindful of our impermanence is a valuable practice. And it doesn't need to be morbid; instead, it can be empowering—a way to intentionally rewrite the script of our life so we live in harmony with who we truly are.

In Buddhism, there is a practice of contemplating death called *maranasati* that is said to create a kind of spiritual urgency. The intention of the practice is to serve as a reminder that death comes without warning so that we come to value the here and now. According to tradition, *maranasati* is an antidote to complacency, prompting us to put forth extraordinary effort, zeal, and enthusiasm. It's a way to jolt ourselves awake and become motivated to seek deeper, more meaningful lives in the present. When we contemplate the fact that our days are numbered, we are motivated to make bolder choices. This spiritual urgency, called *samvega*, is considered a sign that the practice of mindfulness of death has "succeeded."

In *Your Creative Soul*, the audio learning program I was honored to cocreate with author-teacher Caroline Myss, she implored listeners to imagine themselves on their deathbed: "When you say, 'No, what will people think?' that's your signal that maybe you should hit a pause button and say, 'Am I repressing my spirit?' In that moment, I want you to think of yourself dying all alone. Where are all these people that you were thinking about in that moment? 'What will *they* say?' Where are the 'they'? Where are they? Are you with me? They're nowhere. That's exactly how you should think of them. They are nowhere. Then make your decision about whether or not to repress yourself."

If it sounds like I am trying to light a fire under you, dear reader, it's because I am. Practically everything in our current culture tempts us to live a life of mindless distraction. Even now, as you read these words, clickbait may be beckoning you to your smartphone or computer screen. There are people working full time in industries that create these distractions. We need a new kind of effort to move through our days with purpose in this new world in which we live.

Play Your Role Full Out

In 2009, Bronnie Ware wrote an online article called "Regrets of the Dying," based on the time she'd spent working in palliative care. The post spread like wildfire, as people all over the world responded to the wisdom Ware had absorbed in the course of her work, and she went on to write an entire book on the subject, *The Top Five Regrets of the Dying*.

These are the five regrets Ware says she heard most often from patients in their last weeks of life:

1. I wish I'd had the courage to live a life true to myself, not the life others expected of me.
2. I wish I hadn't worked so hard.
3. I wish I'd had the courage to express my feelings.
4. I wish I had stayed in touch with my friends.
5. I wish that I had let myself be happier.

If I had only one wish for you, it would be for you to live out your remaining days in such a way that you'll never have to look back and say, "I wish I'd truly lived." We all have regrets. We all have things we'd like to go back and do differently. But the glory of each new day is that we get to begin again. Each time the curtain rises on a new performance, we get to practice being present and playing our role full out. Whatever is going on for us, whether we're in the midst of joy or sorrow, we can honor the role we've been given by playing our part to the best of our ability. So let's hit a reset button together right now, today, and take a careful look at what truly matters to us. As we approach the final chapter of this book, let's look deeply into our own soul and vow to take direction, for whatever time we have left, from the part of us that knows that all things end.

In a song that will bring any thespian to tears, singer-songwriter Frank Turner sings, "Always take the stage like it's the last night of your life." The extraordinary mindfulness I wish for all of us is that we remember to remember that we have only a nanosecond on the world's stage. Let's not waste it. Instead, let's choose wisely what we will do with the most valuable assets we have: our time and attention. Staying mindful of the fact that our days are numbered can help us be clear-eyed and awake enough to make our moments count for something—to live full out from the core of who we are, not who anyone, including us, thinks we should be.

Questions to Live By

- If you never improved another single thing about yourself, could you love yourself exactly as you are?

- What is center stage in your life right now?

- If you were to die tomorrow, what regrets would you have?

- What will you do with your time on life's stage, knowing that one day—who knows when—the curtain is going to come down?

Chapter 10:

Embrace New Roles

Now I become myself. It's taken
Time, many years and places;
I have been dissolved and shaken.
Worn other people's faces . . .

—May Sarton

One Friday night, as I sat reading on my red sofa, my two dogs snuggled around my feet, I glanced up at the clock and saw it was close to 8:00 p.m. *The Phantom of the Opera* would start soon, thrilling and moving new generations of audiences. Someone was in that dressing room on Forty-fourth Street, warming up her voice and putting on her Christine makeup, and I found myself silently sending her the perspective I wish I'd had when I was in her place: *Stand in your power. Give it your all, and be gentle with yourself. You're enough.*

I set down my book, got up, and walked through the sliding glass doors and onto the back deck outside my New

Jersey condo. I remembered the emotional magnitude of the scene when I took the Phantom's face in my hands and imagined all the love that has ever existed throughout time pouring through me into him—and it struck me that for all my years of seeking, I had failed to notice the great lesson that had been right in front of me six nights a week for ten years, the lesson embodied by the character I'd played.

Now, though, as I looked out at the glittering lights of New York City in the distance, it was as clear as the moon in the cloudless sky before me. We must see life not as we wish it to be—picture perfect, a white mask covering the difficult parts—but as it truly is: beautiful, confounding, achingly impermanent, and brimming with both laughter and tears. When we have the courage to hold all of experience in a compassionate embrace, life is transformed. We become free.

Stop Acting a Part

In his book *Nothing to Do, Nowhere to Go: Waking Up to Who You Are*, Buddhist monk and peace activist Thich Nhat Hanh writes: "The person who has nothing to do is sovereign of herself. She doesn't need to put on airs or leave any trace behind. The true person is an active participant, engaged in her environment while remaining unoppressed by it. She lives in awareness as an ordinary person, whether standing, walking, lying down, or sitting. She doesn't act a part, even the part of a great Zen master."

This idea is not in conflict with passion. In fact, as I experience it, it is the opposite of ennui. Each breath is a new dawn. Hearing the birds sing in the morning is as exquisite as hearing any coloratura's trill on the stage of the Metropolitan Opera.

In our rush to get our daily tasks done, caught up in our frenzied pace, we often forget to notice anything else.

We spend our days ticking off our to-do lists—buying our groceries, driving here and there, trying to get or stay in shape, and doing all we can to maintain clean homes and connected relationships.

Sometimes we keep all the plates spinning rather successfully, and when we do we feel good about ourselves and our lives. Yet even then we thirst for something more. In an honest conversation with a trusted friend, we might admit that we're exhausted and that we fantasize as we stand in line at Whole Foods with our carts full of organic produce about packing it up, à la Elizabeth Gilbert, and eating and praying our way across the globe, or maybe just across the street to give our bodies some love at the holistic spa on the corner. But even if we succumb to temptation and get the massage we're dying for, once we leave the spa and head back to the fray, it isn't long before we find ourselves right back on that hamster wheel.

"Every morning I awaken torn between the desire to save the world and the inclination to savor it," wrote E. B. White. I've talked to many people who experience a similar existential tension. To lie down in the grass on a summer's day like Mary Oliver—this makes our whole body into a song of worship. And yet some of us fear that if we allow our inner inclinations to guide our actions—if we indulge the thing inside us that urges us to lie down in a hammock and simply savor the beauty surrounding us—we will cease all creativity and social interaction and become hermetic, gluttonous, hedonistic ne'er-do-wells.

I used to believe this, too. But I'm learning that the need to create cannot stay dormant for long. We are creative beings. Eventually, we tire of the hammock; eventually, the expressive itch takes hold and presses our fingers to the keyboard or lifts our paintbrush to a canvas or urges our voice into a song. If we don't allow our voices to be *ex*pressed, we may find ourselves becoming *de*pressed. I was so moved when I first learned that Native American medicine men traditionally ask three questions of the sick: *When was the last time you sang? When was the last time you danced? When was the last time you told your story?*

Our inner guidance system is trustworthy and true. When we surrender ourselves to it, we find there is no need to "act a part," and we begin to move through our days from our own center. If we're lucky, we begin to trust our capacity for being and doing.

Redefine Success

If what Thich Nhat Hanh says is true, however, and there is nothing to do and nowhere to go, what, we may wonder, is the point of pursuing our dreams at all? Perhaps the pursuit is about something deeper than getting the thing we think we want. For example, research by Daniel Gilbert, author of *Stumbling on Happiness,* has shown people are not very good at predicting what will make them happy or how long that happiness will last. "They expect positive events to make them much happier than those events actually do, and they expect negative events to make them unhappier than they actually do," said Gilbert in an interview with *Harvard Business Review.* "A recent study showed that very few experiences affect us for more than three months. When good things happen, we celebrate for a while and then sober up. When bad things happen, we weep and whine for a while and then pick ourselves up and get on with it."

Achieving our dreams, then, rarely pays the dividends of happiness and long-term fulfillment we imagine it will when we're starting out. Speaking from my own experience, I was grateful and gratified at the top of the *Phantom* ladder, but my inner confidence never caught up with my external circumstances—and in many ways, my happiness didn't either. There's little that's quite so confusing as reaching the peak of the mountain you've set out to climb. On the one hand, the feeling of being at the top is exhilarating, breathtaking, indescribably exciting. On the other hand, when you're at the top you're completely exposed and vulnerable to the elements—and the only way to go is down.

The moment you realize this—and you realize it very quickly—it becomes difficult to simply enjoy the view. Your every flaw and mistake is on display and if you're anything like me, they become magnified in your mind. But you've reached the pinnacle; you've made it. There's no room for self-pity there. So you enjoy it as best you can—and when you can't, you try to push the sadness away, because to do anything else makes you feel guilty, ungrateful, and unworthy of the success with which you've been blessed. My character could look at the Phantom through eyes of love and compassion when he was unmasked, but I could not do that for myself. At the height of my success, I struggled for a sense of worthiness in a world that tells all of us we need to be not good, not great, but the very best—perfection itself. And I struggled for a sense of fulfillment in a culture that tells all of us that "making it" will make us happy.

If starring in one of the most coveted roles on Broadway for nearly a decade didn't make me feel happy and good enough, I wondered, what would? Before the loss of my father and my health scare, a part of me kept insisting that to continue to be successful meant that I needed to climb higher and do more, but what did that mean? Originate a role, win a Tony, star in TV shows or films, win an Academy Award? Even if I could reach such improbable heights, where would it end? The ego's relentless striving to prove its worth feeds on the ubiquitous and relentless cultural pressure on all of us to climb ever higher. But, having been broken open, I could not ignore the soft recognition of my heart: my quiet yearning was no longer about reaching for the stars. What I longed for had more to do with touching the earth.

So what, then, is the point of pursuing our dreams? What if it's the thorough engagement of our heart? What if it's really about maximizing the gifts we've been given and offering them to the world? What if it's about those crystalline moments of expression when you feel like a conduit, like lightning, when your aliveness is like a force of nature moving through you and touching everything outside of you? What if it's about being an open vessel for all that is larger than us to pour through? Following our aliveness may lead us down unexpected paths.

In 2015, Patrick Pichette, Google's CFO at the time, decided to leave his position in order to spend more time with his family. "I love my job (still do), my colleagues, my friends, the opportunities to lead and change the world," he wrote in his moving and honest exit memo, which he posted to Google+. "In the end, life is wonderful, but nonetheless a series of trade offs, especially between business/professional endeavours and family/community. And thankfully, I feel I'm at a point in my life where I no longer have to make such tough choices anymore."

Pichette loved his job, but he also loved his family—and he recognized that it was time to change the balance of how much he was giving to each. Not all of us are in a financial position to make this kind of choice, of course, but redefining success does not necessarily mean quitting your job. The point here is that Pichette recognized something that all of us would be wise to keep in mind: real success means not missing out on your life. Either we can stand in the wings and watch, or we can make a decision to take center stage and play the leading role in our own life story.

Unmask What Matters

Randy Pausch, author of *The Last Lecture*, was forty-six years old when he discovered he was dying of pancreatic cancer. "Life," he said after his diagnosis, "is 10 percent black, 10 percent white, and 80 percent gray."

The 80-percent-gray argument seemed to me an easy one to make if you were someone who had been dealt a fair hand in life. But here was a man whose doctors told him he had maybe three months to live, and he had decided not only that 80 percent of life was gray but also that gray was beautiful.

A year after I left *Phantom*, facing a tumor diagnosis and the loss of my beloved father, I felt as though I'd been ushered through a baptism of self and all that remained was a commitment to fully inhabit my time on Earth, fully communicate the love I feel, and be as present as possible as often as possible. In that open place emerged a tenderness that has yet to recede.

For a time, of course, all I wanted to do was take a Xanax and crawl under the covers. I did that on occasion. But the more I went straight to the source of my pain—my own interior—the better I came to know its landscape. It was not unique. It looked just like everyone else's: 10 percent white, 10 percent black, 80 percent gray. And I discovered that when I remember to honor the truth of my experience and practice self-care—to slow down, breathe, take in the beauty around me—that gray takes on every color of the rainbow. I learned that pain, fully experienced, rises, crests, and recedes like waves in an ocean. Those waves drop us down to a deeper level of living—closer to the heart of things, closer to what matters.

Moving through the waves of our experience gives us more empathy and compassion for ourselves and those around us. Of course, being human, we forget what we know. We can't live every moment of our lives in the deep. The challenge, then, when we get caught up in busyness and distracted by the trivial, is to remind ourselves to stay close to the things that matter and to clear the decks of the things that don't.

Clear the Decks
Self-inquiry for staying close to what matters

To keep myself on track, I frequently ask myself these three questions:
- Do the people I love know how much they mean to me?
- Am I present to the miracle in front of me, whether it's a pair of eyes, a computer screen, or a sunset?
- Am I following my aliveness wherever it leads?

Try asking yourself these questions—or, if these don't feel quite right for you, come up with a few of your own. What are some questions you can keep returning to that will guide you in the direction of what matters most to you?

Shed Your Old Skin

"The only man I know who behaves sensibly is my tailor," George Bernard Shaw once wrote. "He takes my measurements anew each time he sees me. The rest go on with their old measurements and expect me to fit them." Nietzsche, meanwhile, cautioned, "The snake that cannot shed its skin perishes." Growth and change are essential, and unavoidable, parts of life. At some point, we all have to shed the skin that's become too restrictive.

This does not mean that we should always be looking for the next best thing. In contrast, the new paradigm of success, if we are wise, will be not about "bigger, better, more" but about living wholeheartedly as you. No longer a life of endless striving but a life of endless practice—at being completely here, completely you, with nothing separating you from your direct experience of being alive.

Each one of us has been summoned on a soul level for a purpose that is greater than we are. Every person is born with gifts. And new callings give us new ways to let our gifts meet the needs of the world.

As my time in *Phantom* drew to a close, I had a deep inner knowing that not only was it time to say good-bye to Christine; it was time to say good-bye to Broadway. When I tell you this was a major personal crisis, I am not being hyperbolic. Musicals were my first love and what I'd trained my whole life to do. But the identity of singer/ actress felt like an old costume that no longer fit. In retrospect, it's clear to me that I stayed in the role longer than I should have—certainly with regard to my own well being. Toward the end of my run, I was frequently missing shows because I so desperately needed mental health days. The adrenal burnout and emotional and physical fatigue made me feel like I was walking around with a dark cloud over my head; even the cocktail of antidepressants I was taking offered little relief. But I stayed because the fear of leaving was so great. In my soul, I knew that my Broadway journey was complete; the aliveness had gone out of it for me. But what would I do next? I had no way of knowing if, when, or how I could earn a living or find fulfillment outside of theater. The thought of leaving behind the only profession I'd ever known was terrifying.

Willingly entering the chrysalis phase is not easy for any of us. If you're in the midst of a transition, my heart goes out to you. You might be feeling some of the same things I did: anxiety about the future, self-doubt about starting over, desperation to hurry up the process and become that butterfly now. The waiting and not knowing can be agonizing. But we cannot speed up the process any more than a caterpillar can; it actually has to dissolve completely into a sticky goo of nothing before it grows a new self and emerges ready to fly. If you're in the messy middle, take heart. Transitions are tough, but by their very nature, they don't last forever.

My own chrysalis phase was slow, confusing, frightening, and fraught. As with my journey to Broadway, it took a long time and a lot of false starts before I found my voice and my way. When I first left the show, I pretty much just wanted to take a nap for a few years. But all the while I felt a background pressure to figure out what my next career would entail. I prayed, journaled, meditated, and asked for guidance. I did everything I knew to do, and, for what felt like far too long, no answers came. But one night, alone in a hotel room, I felt something grab me by the heart in a way I hadn't experienced since I'd seen *Annie* as a child. In one of those rare-but-wonderful "download" moments, a scene that simultaneously excited and frightened me played out in my mind: I was onstage speaking and singing in front of an audience, but I wasn't wearing a costume or playing a character; I was just being me, and I was telling my story. I was talking about how my own fear and self-doubt almost held me back from going after what I most wanted. I was sharing what I thought might help others believe in themselves and pursue their passions.

After that "download," I tried to figure out to whom I might speak. I thought my message could serve high school students who wanted to pursue the arts, so I started there. Being myself onstage with no character to hide behind and no tried-and-true script brought me a whole new slew of OS!Ms. But as I shared my story, invitations began coming seemingly out of nowhere—and no matter how many old fears whispered, *This is too big for you. Who do you think you are?* I kept saying yes.

I really do believe that when you follow your heart, the universe rises up to support you. I never could have imagined then that those early speaking engagements would eventually lead to keynote addresses delivered to rooms full of professionals at the top of the Million Dollar Round Table, at conferences filled with Fortune 500 executives, at associations and charity galas, from New York City to Silicon Valley and beyond.

I can honestly say that this unexpectedly wonderful second act I'm in the midst of is the most rewarding one yet. I was so fortunate to see a big dream come true. It is incredibly gratifying to now have the opportunity to share what that journey taught me in hopes of inspiring others to dream bigger dreams for themselves.

When I talk to people about my decision to leave the business, they sometimes look at me with bewilderment or, worse, disappointment. "How could you walk away from Broadway?" they demand. "Don't you miss it?" Some seem perplexed, or even woeful on my behalf. Many are full of advice about what I should be doing now. But at this point in my life, I try to avoid buying into shoulds. We are each tasked with creating our lives from the inside out and living in accordance with our most deeply held values.

My husband and I moved to San Diego in 2016. We live in a quiet condo surrounded by trees. I'm still performing, but in a different way now, as a keynote speaker–singer (yep, it's a thing). I'm also a frequent "inspir-tainer" at client appreciation parties with financial advisors and business owners. I'm still singing all those Christine songs, sometimes with symphonies, sometimes at private parties and corporate events. I frequently perform as a solo artist, and I have the great pleasure of doing concerts with friends who have starred in other well-known Broadway shows. On extra-special occasions, I still get to perform opposite my favorite Phantom, my husband, Ron. I sometimes lead retreats and facilitate workshops as well. It's all a blessing.

But I also treasure my time at home these days. I spent so long learning how to be visible and "out there." Now life is teaching me how to be content "in here" while still contributing in a way that is meaningful to me. In my twenties, I never would have believed I could be so happy staring up at trees, needing nothing more than the sight of a hummingbird to make my day.

The best part of this new chapter of life I've entered into is that I get to be the real me. My real essence has a lot more time to play. Both onstage and off, I get to be more of who I truly am—and that is a person whom I have finally learned, at least most of the time, to befriend.

We are taught that what matters is to see our name in lights, but what I wish for you to know deeply is that your name has already been written in The Book of Life. There is nothing you need to do, create, achieve, or become in order to "make it." You've already won the prize: you're here. Your being you makes our hearts sing. Trust this. Know this. There is no greater role to play in a lifetime than the one in which you have been cast. This is the role you have been waiting for, the one that proves you are enough. It has already been given to you. Please accept your Oscar, your Tony, your Lifetime Achievement Award now, because bravo, my friend—you got the gig, and you are perfect in the role of you.

Questions to Live By

- Where are you now internally? Are you living outgrown roles or wearing old masks? What old measurements do you or others use that no longer fit?

- What do others say to you that makes you feel as though you need to wear a mask?

- What do you say to yourself that makes you feel you need to show up a certain way?

- What could you say to yourself to give yourself the permission, courage, and perspective to be able to show up the way you most want to today?

- What does success really look like for you now?

Appendix:

Unmasking Practices—
a Quick Reference Guide

Throughout this book, I've included exercises that I personally find useful. I have gathered them all here for easy reference. Please utilize whatever speaks to you and leave the rest.

Mirroring Love

A practice of harnessing the power of your own loving heart and turning that love toward yourself

1. Imagine someone you love fiercely. Gather your lion/lioness energy. Whom would you protect with all your might?

2. Imagine that someone harmed that person and they came to you feeling wounded. How would you respond? Think about the power of your love—the force field you can create with your own loving heart. Let yourself feel it.

3. Turn your fierce, loving heart toward itself like a mirror is being held up in front of you and reflecting all of that love back to you. Turn the power of your loving heart toward itself. Speak to yourself the way you would speak to a hurting child. Touch your hand the way you would touch the hand of someone you care about when they are suffering. Hold your own hand—literally—the way you would hold the hand of someone you love when they are gripped by fear or sadness, in that gesture that says, *I'm here for you. I've got you. We'll get through this together. I love you.*

4. Sit with the power of this love. Feel its healing energy.

As the Buddha said, "You could search the whole world and never find anyone as deserving of love as yourself."

Heart Inquiry
A practice of excavating important truths from the wisest place within you

HeartMath has developed a number of tools and techniques for tapping into the heart's intelligence. I've used their technologies for many years and have found them to be game-changers. Here's my variation on one of my favorite HeartMath tools:

1. Sit quietly and close your eyes.

2. Place both hands over your heart and breathe a little more deeply than you normally do—five to six seconds on each inhalation and exhalation. Imagine your breath is traveling into and out of your heart.

3. Imagine your mind slowly traveling down and curling up like a cat in your chest.

4. Ask your heart for guidance.

5. When you feel ready, open your eyes and get out your journal. Write for ten minutes, beginning with the following prompts:
   - "When I really listen inwardly, what I hear is . . ."
   - "If I'm really honest, what I yearn for is . . ."
   - "In a quiet corner of my heart, I know that . . ."

Focus On Your Heart's Desire

A practice of tuning in to your desires—and realizing them*

Sandra Selby's *The Five Minute Positive Focus Daily Journal* is a self-reflection journal that asks readers to take five minutes out of each day to answer the same set of questions. I've used this book for several years, and I've found that it's a wonderful morning ritual—a pleasurable, quick, and easy way to hear your inner voice and connect with your inner wisdom. Selby presents five questions in her journal, but here we'll focus on just two: "Divine Desires and Dreams" and "Positive Intention for Today."

1. Divine Desires and Dreams—What Is My "Heart's Desire"?

This question is about your dreams and desires of *all* sizes. We all have *big* dreams, as well as everyday, smaller desires. Put it all down, and repeat them as often as you would like . . . or do a new one every day. You can put down exactly what you would like to happen, or what you would like something to look like when it is complete. This will take the emotionality out of it, and the fears. Imagine that this is a perfect world and that you can have whatever you want. What would that be?

Example: "I see myself getting the job of my dreams—one that is both fulfilling and challenging."

2. Positive Intention for Today—A Step Toward My Dreams!

This is your action step. You are putting your energy where your dreams are . . . and the universe will meet you tenfold. Make this step easy to handle, and you may end up adding other steps to it. Do not let yourself get overwhelmed with huge, unrealistic assignments that will stop the positive process before it has begun.

Example: "I will apply to one new job today that seems like a good fit for me."

Try devoting five minutes a day to this practice. You'll be amazed at how much easier it will make it for you to hear your inner voice when it has something to say!

*Adapted with permission from Sandra Selby.

Engage the Oppressor

A practice of giving voice to what holds you back so your gifts and capacities no longer remain stuck inside you

1. In your journal, describe what holds you back from fully expressing your voice. Give it form. Personify it. Anthropomorphize it. Express it in nature images, color, texture. Begin with "My fear (or silence/stuckness/hesitation) is . . ." What does it look, sound, taste like? What does it do? Don't think, just write, and see where the pen takes you.

Examples: "My fear is a sixth-grade boy who sticks his foot out and laughs as my face hits the gravel and my bottom lip bleeds."

"My silence is a desert with no heat, a vast emptiness with no life in sight and no one to hear my cries for help or my song."

2. Turn toward and talk to your oppressor. Ask it what it wants you to know.

Example: "Why are you keeping me stuck? What do I need to understand?"

The answer you get might be kind or harsh: "I'm just trying to keep you safe." Or "You don't deserve to be heard."

3. Next, describe the opposite of your fear/silence/stuckness. What qualities are present? What do you see, smell, taste, touch, hear?

Example: "A golden light like the surface of the sun with beautiful rays pointing in all directions, warm, bright, like luminosity itself. A golden flame like a shield, an angel's harp. It surrounds my body and keeps the darkness from being able to touch me."

4. Turn toward the opposite force and let it speak to you.

Example: "I am the barrier between you and all forces of darkness and shame. I will surround you and fill your body and carry you forward when you're too fearful to move on your own. I am stronger than your ego, your self-image, your susceptibility to criticism. You are a part of me and all that is. Hold tight to me, and I will protect you. You are safe. I've got you. I've got this."

Your Ideal Self

A practice of checking whether your ideal self is grounded in reality*

Take a moment to reflect on these three questions:
1. What is my ideal self? And why is it so? Is it based on early experiences when I was helpless and dependent on the love and appreciation of others to cope with life?

2. Is it realistic? In a world of billions of others, can I truly be the smartest, most beautiful, most loved or faultless person there is? Is there even such a person—or am I, as a human, forgetting that my imperfections are what make me perfect?

3. Is it achievable? Is it aligned with my inherent strengths and weaknesses, or am I desperately pursuing a mirage? Because unless your ideal self is grounded in your unique reality, you will not be able to rise to your highest potential.

*This exercise is excerpted from writing by Homaira Kabir, with her permission.

Dr. Kristin Neff's Self-Compassion Break

A practice of giving ourselves the same kindness and care we'd give to a good friend in a stressful situation*

According to Dr. Neff, self-compassion has three important elements: mindfulness vs. over-identification, common humanity vs. isolation, and self-kindness vs. self-judgment.

Think of a situation in your life that is difficult, that is causing you stress. Call the situation to mind, and see if you can actually feel the stress and emotional discomfort in your body. Now, say to yourself:

1. This is a moment of suffering. That's mindfulness. Other options include:
- This hurts.
- Ouch.
- This is stress.

2. Suffering is a part of life. That's common humanity. Other options include:

- Other people feel this way.
- I'm not alone.
- We all struggle in our lives.

Now, put your hands over your heart; feel the warmth of your hands and the gentle touch of your hands on your chest. Or adopt any soothing touch that feels right for you.

3. May I be kind to myself. Ask yourself, "What do I need to hear right now to express kindness to myself?" Is there a phrase that speaks to you in your particular situation? Consider these:
- May I give myself the compassion that I need.
- May I learn to accept myself as I am.
- May I forgive myself.
- May I be strong.
- May I be patient.

This practice can be used any time of day or night, and will help you remember to evoke the three aspects of self-compassion when you need it most.

*Used with permission from Dr. Kristin Neff.

Conversation Observation

A practice of observing yourself when you are most "you," so you can bring your authentic essence to high-pressure situations

1. The next time you're talking to someone you feel completely confident around—maybe it's your spouse or your best friend—bring up a topic you're passionate about or a story you want to share with them.

2. As you're talking, practice dual awareness: Let one part of your mind be the witness to your experience. Observe your authentic communication style. Begin to notice, *This is my tone when I'm confident and passionate. This is the way I gesture. This is what my body language is like.*

3. The next time you're in a high-stakes situation, see if you can inhabit those same qualities and characteristics. You are rehearsing being relaxed, open, and thoroughly yourself so that in high-stakes situations you have a point of reference that can help you re-create your authentic communication style.

Connection Reflection

A practice of inwardly connecting with the people you love and extending that love outward through loving-kindness meditation

Meditation can feel like a chore sometimes, another thing on your to-do list that you may not get to in a day and then judge yourself for skipping. LKM transformed my own relationship with meditation. (Full disclosure: there were actually two things that contributed to the shift for me: practicing LKM and simultaneously using an app created by HeartMath called Inner Balance.) It turned what used to be a "should" into something I actually look forward to doing. It isn't boring! You get to contemplate the positive qualities in people and wish them well. I usually start out with a goal of practicing for only ten minutes, but it feels so wonderful that I often end up staying with it far longer.

It's no surprise that research shows a multitude of physiological benefits to this practice. When I read Barbara Fredrickson's research, I found it so exciting that it became a huge motivator for me to start doing LKM daily. Here's my slight variation on LKM, a practice I call Connection Reflection. This practice works for me, but please feel free to play around with the steps and use your own phrases to see what works best for you:

1. Sit comfortably and close your eyes. Breathe a little more deeply than you normally would. Imagine your breath going into and out of your heart area.

2. Bring to mind someone who cares about you. It need not be a perfect relationship, but think of someone who truly cares about your well-being. Let the feeling of being cared about warm your heart.

3. Now bring to mind someone you love. Think about the good qualities that person embodies. Silently wish them well, using your own version of the four classic phrases of LKM, staying with each phrase for one full in-and-out breath. Here are the phrases I use:
   • May you be peaceful and happy.
   • May you be healthy and filled with vitality.
   • May you be safe from internal and external harm.
   • May you live with ease and joy.

4. Continue the practice with other people you love or anyone you know who could use some positive thoughts. Next, think of a neutral person—the cashier at the grocery store, perhaps. Wish them the above.

5. Wish yourself each of the four phrases.

It's important to include yourself in LKM. You can begin with yourself, if you like, but you may find it easier to "warm up" your heart by sending loving-kindness to people you care about first.

You can continue wishing the four phrases to as many people as you like. Consider ending by zooming out and wishing that your entire community, state, country, or even the planet or all sentient beings will be happy, healthy, safe, and peaceful.

Gather Your Spiritual Support

A practice of actively becoming more aware of the many ways in which you are supported

1. Sit quietly and close your eyes.

2. Feel how the surface you are sitting on is supporting you. Notice how your musculoskeletal structure is supporting you. As you breathe, feel how all the air you need is there for you.

3. Bring to mind someone who cares about you. It may not be a perfect relationship, but think of a person who cares about your well-being. Let the feeling of being cared for fill your heart. Call to mind anyone—whether you know them personally or not—who would encourage you to live the truest expression of who you are. Think of ancestors, spiritual leaders, counselors or therapists, authors, mentors, teachers, or anyone else who gives you a sense of being supported toward the life you want.

4. Imagine them standing in a circle around you. In your mind's eye, look around the circle and make eye contact with each person. What does each one have to say to you?

5. Spend a few minutes with your journal, writing down anything that these inner-support team members shared.

Find the Gift
A practice of cultivating fresh eyes

This is a daylong practice of intentionally looking at the world through fresh eyes. (Side effects may include being filled with love and gratitude.)

1. First thing in the morning, notice everything in your environment that someone else has given to you.

2. Throughout this one entire day, train your brain to find the gifts you've been given.

3. Repeat as often as you can.

Variation: For one full day, notice everything that's going right. Imagine if you woke up and got in the shower and found that the water wouldn't turn on. Then you went to get your morning coffee and the coffeepot had spilled all over the counter. You got in your car and the car wouldn't start. You would notice all of these things—so, instead, try noticing all of the things that *do* go your way. Whether it's technology that works or your timing being just right at important moments, there are sure to be many things that happen as you want them to in a day. Remember to take in the good as you move through this exercise.

Jon Kabat-Zinn's Raisin Consciousness Technique
A practice of bringing mindfulness to whatever we're doing to amplify our performance and keep things from becoming rote

1. Sit comfortably in a chair.

2. Place a raisin in your hand.

3. Examine the raisin as if you have never seen it before.

4. Imagine it as its "plump self" growing on the vine, sur-rounded by nature.

5. As you look at the raisin, become conscious of what you see: the shape, texture, color, size. Is it hard or soft?

6. Bring the raisin to your nose and smell it.

7. Are you anticipating eating the raisin? Is it difficult not to just pop it in your mouth?

8. How does the raisin feel? How small it is in your hand?

9. Place the raisin in your mouth. Become aware of what your tongue is doing.

10. Bite ever so lightly into the raisin. Feel its squishiness.

11. Chew three times and then stop.

12. Describe the flavor of the raisin. What is the texture?

As you make your way through each step of this exer-cise, you'll find that it's like you're seeing, feeling, smelling, and tasting the raisin for the first time. Now that you know how to do this, bring the same awareness and attention to other things in your life!

The Perspective Box

A practice of adjusting your vision to help yourself gain perspective when you need it most

Create a Perspective Box—for yourself or someone else, either a physical one or a virtual one, perhaps in the form of a file on your computer.

What to put in it:

- An "achievements" list: What have you accomplished in your life thus far? What big achievements can you lay claim to? What about the small ones?
- An "obstacles overcome" list: What difficulties have you surmounted in your life? What challenges have you faced? (Acknowledge how hard you've tried. Effort matters more than results.)
- Thank-you notes you've received (also make a note of verbal thanks, handshakes, pats on the back, et cetera)
- Your mission statement: What are your most important reasons for doing what you're doing?

Going forward: At the end of each day, write down: 1) three ways your efforts today made a difference or will make a difference to another person or group of people; 2) three things you did well today; 3) three times you felt loved, acknowledged, or included today. Put it all in your Perspective Box.

Drop the Rope

A practice of experiencing the witnessing presence that holds all aspects of your self

1. Hold out your hands, palms facing the sky.

2. Imagine in your left hand the "you" who strives for improvement, the taskmaster who insists you should be the perfect size, the best at everything you do, and so on.

3. Imagine in your right hand the "you" who insists you'll never get it right, the one who tells you you'll never be good enough, you shouldn't even try, and so on.

4. "See" the inner taskmaster in the left hand and the inner flagellator in the right.

5. Now, as you gaze back and forth at these two opposing sides, ask yourself, "Who is the one doing the holding?" Can the observing presence—the larger you who is witnessing both aspects—love both extremes? Can you drop the rope in the tug-of-war and be the loving presence that holds it all?

Clear the Decks

Self-inquiry for staying close to what matters

To keep myself on track, I frequently ask myself these three questions:
- Do the people I love know how much they mean to me?
- Am I present to the miracle in front of me, whether it's a pair of eyes, a computer screen, or a sunset?
- Am I following my aliveness wherever it leads?

Try asking yourself these questions—or, if these don't feel quite right for you, come up with a few of your own. What are some questions you can keep returning to that will guide you in the direction of what matters most to you?

Endnotes

Introduction

J. Maureen Henderson, "One in Four Millennials Would Quit Their Job to Be Famous," *Forbes*, January 24, 2017, https://www.forbes.com/sites/jmaureenhenderson/2017/01/24/one-in-four-millennials-would quit their job to be famous/#741093562c43.

Chapter 1

Hara Estroff Marano, "Our Brain's Negative Bias," *Psychology Today*, June 20, 2003, https://www.psychologytoday.com/articles/200306/our-brains-negative-bias.

Rick Hanson, PhD, "Take In the Good," June 1, 2017, http://www.rickhanson.net/take-in-the-good.

Thomas Merton, *Conjectures of a Guilty Bystander* (New York: Image, 1968).

Chapter 2

Francis P. Cholle, "What Is Intuition, and How Do We Use It?" *Psychology Today*, August 31, 2011, https://www. psychologytoday.com/blog/the-intuitive-compass/201108/ what-is-intuition-and-how-do-we-use-it.

HeartMath, "Intuition Research: Coherence and the Surprising Role of the Heart," https://www.heartmath.org/ research/science-of-the-heart/intuition-research.

Shané Schutte, "Ignoring Your Instincts Will Be the Wrong Decision in 3 out of 4 Cases," *Real Business*, January 1, 2015, http://realbusiness.co.uk/hr-and-management/2015/01/21/ ignoring-your-instincts-will-be-the-wrong-decision-in-3-out-of-4-cases.

Chapter 3

Elton John, interview with Terry Gross, *Fresh Air*, NPR, January 1, 2014, http://www.npr.org/templates/transcript/ transcript.php?storyId=256607935.

Jaruwan Sakulku and James Alexander, "The Impostor Phenomenon," *International Journal of Behavioral Science*, 2011, http://bsris.swu.ac.th/journal/i6/6-6_Jaruwan_73-92. pdf.

Tavi Gevinson, "I Want It to Be Worth It: An Interview with Emma Watson," *Rookie*, May 27, 2013, http://www. rookiemag.com/2013/05/emma-watson-interview.

Chapter 4

Amy Morin, "Science Explains the Link Between Self-Compassion and Success," Forbes, October 1, 2015, https://www.

forbes.com/sites/amymorin/2015/10/01/science-explains-the-link-between-self-compassion-and-success/#6999b9752384.

Carol Dweck, *Mindset: The New Psychology of Success* (New York: Ballantine Books, 2007).

Kristin Neff, "The Space Between Self-Esteem and Self-Compassion," *YouTube*, February 6, 2013, https://www.youtube.com/watch?v=IvtZBUSplr4.

Marina Krakovsky, "Self-Compassion Fosters Mental Health," *Scientific American*, July 1, 2012, https://www.scientificamerican.com/article/self-compassion-fosters-mental-health.

Chapter 5

Antonio Damasio, *Descartes' Error: Emotion, Reason, and the Human Brain* (New York: Penguin, 2005).

Brené Brown, *Daring Greatly. How the Courage to Be Vulnerable Transforms the Way We Live, Love, Parent, and Lead* (New York: Avery, 2015).

"Facts and Statistics," Anxiety and Depression Association of America, accessed September 28, 2017, https://adaa.org/about-adaa/press-room/facts-statistics.

Kat Koppett, *Training to Imagine: Practical Improvisational Theatre Techniques for Trainers and Managers to Enhance Creativity, Teamwork, Leadership, and Learning* (Sterling, VA: Stylus Publishing, 2012).

Seth Godin, *Leap First: Creating Work That Matters* (New York: Sounds True, 2015).

Chapter 6

Barbara L. Fredrickson et al., "Open Hearts Build Lives: Positive Emotions, Induced Through Loving-Kindness Meditation, Build Consequential Personal Resources," August 2008, *Journal of Personality and Social Psychology*, https://www.ncbi.nlm.nih.gov/pmc/articles/PMC3156028.

Liz Mineo, "Good Genes Are Nice, but Joy Is Better," *Harvard Gazette*, April 11, 2017, https://news.harvard.edu/gazette/story/2017/04/over-nearly-80-years-harvard-study-has-been-showing-how-to-live-a-healthy-and-happy-life.

"Random Acts of Kindness," Greater Good Science Center at the University of California, Berkeley, accessed September 28, 2017, http://ggia.berkeley.edu/practice/random_acts_of_kindness#data-tab-why_you_should_try_it.

Robert Waldinger, "What Makes a Good Life? Lessons from the Longest Study on Happiness," TED, November 2015, https://www.ted.com/talks/robert_waldinger_what_makes_a_good_life_lessons_from_the_longest_study_on_happiness/transcript?language=en.

S. Katherine Nelson et al., "Do unto Others or Treat Yourself? The Effects of Prosocial and Self-Focused Behavior on Psychological Flourishing," *Emotion*, September 2016, https://www.ncbi.nlm.nih.gov/pubmed/27100366.

Chapter 7

Amy Elisa Jackson, "We Just Can't Unplug: 2 in 3 Employees Report Working While on Vacation," Glassdoor blog, May 4, 2017, https://www.glassdoor.com/blog/vacation-realities-2017.

Bum Jin Park et al., "The Physiological Effects of Shinrin-Yoku (Taking in the Forest Atmosphere or Forest Bathing): Evidence from Field Experiments in 24 Forests Across Japan," *Environmental Health and Prevention Medicine*, January 2010, https://www.ncbi.nlm.nih.gov/pubmed/19568835.

Ellen J. Langer, *On Becoming an Artist: Reinventing Yourself Through Mindful Creativity* (New York: Ballantine Books, 2006).

Helen Pearson, "Doctors Examine Art," *Nature*, September 12, 2001, http://www.nature.com/news/2001/010913/full/news010913-11.html#B1.

Jim Loehr and Tony Schwartz, *The Power of Full Engagement* (New York: Free Press, 2003).

Patricia Ryan Madson, *Improv Wisdom: Don't Prepare, Just Show Up* (New York: Bell Tower, 2005).

Pema Chödrön, *Comfortable with Uncertainty: 108 Teachings on Cultivating Fearlessness and Compassion* (Boulder: Shambhala, 2003).

Quentin Fottrell, "The Sad Reason Half of Americans Don't Take All Their Paid Vacation," *MarketWatch*, May 28, 2017, http://www.marketwatch.com/story/55-of-american workers-dont-take-all-their-paid-vacation-2016-06-15.

Shawn Achor and Michelle Gielan, "The Data-Driven Case for Vacation," *Harvard Business Review*, July 13, 2016, https://hbr.org/2016/07/the-data-driven-case-for-vacation.

Stuart Brown and Christopher Vaughan, *Play: How It Shapes the Brain, Opens the Imagination, and Invigorates the Soul* (New York: Avery, 2010).

Chapter 8

Adam Grant and Jane Dutton, "Beneficiary or Benefactor: Are People More Prosocial When They Reflect on Receiving or Giving?," http://journals.sagepub.com/doi/abs/10.1177/0956797612439424.

Amy Wrzesniewski et al., "Multiple Types of Motives Don't Multiply the Motivation of West Point Cadets," *Proceedings of the National Academy of Sciences of the United States of America*, July 29, 2014, https://www.ncbi.nlm.nih.gov/pmc/articles/PMC4121823.

Brent D. Rosso et al., "On the Meaning of Work: A Theoretical Integration and Review," *Research in Organizational Behavior*, November 2010, http://www.sciencedirect.com/science/article/pii/S0191308510000067.

Daniel H. Pink, *Drive: The Surprising Truth About What Motivates Us* (New York: Riverhead Books, 2011).

"Human Potential and Happiness: An Interview with Richard Davidson," 1440 Multiversity, July 12, 2017, https://1440.org/human-potential-and-happiness-an-interview-with-richard-davidson.

Leil Lowndes, *How to Talk to Anyone: 92 Little Tricks for Big Success in Relationships* (New York: McGraw-Hill Education, 2003).

Melissa Dahl, "If You Can't Have the Job You Love, Love the Job You Have," *New York*, April 11, 2016, http://nymag.com/scienceofus/2016/04/if-you-cant-have-the-job-you-love-love-the-job-you-have.html.

Simon Sinek, *Start with Why: How Great Leaders Inspire Everyone to Take Action* (New York: Portfolio, December 2011).

Tad Friend, "Jumpers," *New Yorker*, October 13, 2003, https://www.newyorker.com/magazine/2003/10/13/jumpers.

Chapter 9

Bronnie Ware, *The Top Five Regrets of the Dying: A Life Transformed by the Dearly Departed* (Carlsbad, CA: Hay House, 2012).

Chapter 10

Patrick Pichette, Google+ post, March 10, 2015, https://plus.google.com/+PatrickPichette/posts/8Khr5LnKtub.

"The Science Behind the Smile," *Harvard Business Review*, February 2012, https://hbr.org/2012/01/the-science-behind-the-smile.

Thich Nhat Hanh, *Nothing to Do, Nowhere to Go: Waking Up to Who You Are* (Berkeley: Parallax Press, 2007).

Comps For You

www.sandrajoseph.com/bookgifts

I'm excited to share some wonderful complimentary resources with you to help weave the lessons from this book into your daily life:

- A downloadable *Unmasking What Matters* journal with highlights from each of the ten lessons in the book.
- A fast and effective online process for eliminating a belief that holds you back such as "I'm not good enough" (from the Lefkoe Method mentioned in Chapter 1).
- A downloadable MP3 of the Peak Performance Paraliminal (mentioned in Chapter 5) to help you rise to your personal best.

Information about Sandra's **keynotes, concerts, workshops,** and **retreats** can be found at **www.sandrajoseph.com**.

A Heartfelt Standing
Ovation of Thanks

This book has been ten years in the making. It would take another ten years to adequately express my appreciation to the many people who helped me along the way. I will start by saying thank you . . .

To my literary agents, Jo-Lynne Worley and Joanie Shoemaker: it's an honor to work with you and a joy to call you friends.

To the team at She Writes Press: for your commitment to helping women tell their stories.

To my publisher, Brooke Warner: for years of encouragement, buoying, and compassionate, expert guidance.

To my editor, Krissa Lagos: for your extraordinary talent, patience, steadfastness, and hustle. I could not have asked for a better companion by my side. You are a writer's dream.

To Annie Tucker: for your attention to detail and careful copyediting.

To Lorraine Ash: for being book doula and soul sister from "Women Writing by the Sea" to the home stretch of this book, and for sending encouraging words and track changes when I needed them most.

To Judith Lindbergh: for your grace and guidance, and to the members of your writer's group, especially Stuart Lutz.

To the many who read my early writing: Martha Beck, Nancy Smith, Julie Cook, Arielle Ford, Elizabeth Lyon, Elisabeth Weed, Sarah Saffian, Brookes Nohlgren, and more, for the new kind of voice lessons you gave me.

To the Phamily: for an amazing ride.

To the Transformational Leadership Council and Association of Transformational Leaders SoCal: for lifting us all higher.

To Pete Bissonette, Learning Strategies, Shelly Lefkoe, The Lefkoe Institute, Howard Martin, Deborah Rozman, HeartMath Institute, and Marci Shimoff: for your generosity of spirit.

To Sam Horn: for modeling what it means to live in accordance with what matters.

To Dr. Rick Hanson: for your kind heart and wise teachings.

To Barbara Thompson: for believing I had something to say and helping me walk through the vulnerability of saying it.

To my family and friends, too numerous to name one by one, especially Josephs, Taorminas, Pasvants, Setchells, Keffers, RoBeates, Ty, Jill, Melissa, Christopher, Seth, Carter, Roger, Joey, Emily, Michael John, Cassidy, Cat, Austen: you fill my heart with gratitude.

To my anam cara, Mark Nepo: for seeing me, for being you, for embodying an unmasked life. Your teachings are my most cherished life lessons.

To Susan Owen: LMFS.

To Rex Nockengust and Gene Allen: for teaching me other-centeredness every day. From your couch on 96th and Columbus to San Diego to the ends of the earth, I will follow you.

To Scott Calcagno: for decades of meeting me in the dark and helping me back into the light. Your creative genius is a gift to me, to this book, and to the world.

To my late father, John Joseph: for teaching me that what matters most is not what you do, but who you are.

To my beautiful mother, Geri Joseph: for your tender heart and resilient spirit and for always saying, "I love you and I'm proud of you." The goodness you see in me is truly a reflection of you.

To my sister, Monica Setchell, my constant, my heart, my person: for keeping me grounded and helping me fly from the very beginning. Your support is everything. I love you.

And to Ron Bohmer, my Superman, my husband, my leading man, my love: for all the times you nudged me forward when I was ready to give up, for being my first reader and biggest champion, for reminding me again and again that "it's all getting done; it's all working out," for your artistry and integrity and your deeply-held conviction that to make a hat matters. Without you, this book would not exist.

Finally, to seekers and dreamers and creators of every kind: for your courage and your voice. You inspire me.

About the Author

Sandra Joseph is a history-making Broadway star. Her legendary run as Christine Daaé in *The Phantom of the Opera* spanned ten years and more than 1,300 performances, and earned her the record as the longest-running leading lady in the longest-running Broadway show of all time. She has been seen on numerous national broadcasts, including *The Oprah Winfrey Show*, CNN, *The Today Show*, *Dateline*, *The Early Show*, *The View*, and *Oprah: Where Are They Now?*

Today, Sandra is on a mission to empower other people's voices through her work as an author, speaker, and workshop facilitator. She is a member of The Transformational Leadership Council, a group of 100 top thought leaders founded by Jack Canfield. She is also the coauthor, with five-time *New York Times* best-selling author Caroline Myss, of *Your Creative Soul: Expressing Your Authentic Voice*. She is married to her costar from *The Phantom of the Opera*, actor Ron Bohmer. They currently reside in Southern California.

Visit her at www.sandrajoseph.com.

Selected Titles from She Writes Press

She Writes Press is an independent publishing
company founded to serve women writers everywhere.
Visit us at www.shewritespress.com.

Note to Self: A Seven-Step Path to Gratitude and Growth by
Laurie Buchanan. $16.95, 978-1-63152-113-3. Transforming
intention into action, *Note to Self* equips you to shed your bag-
gage, bridging the gap between where you are and where you
want to be—body, mind, and spirit—and empowering you to
step into joy-filled living now!

Think Better. Live Better. 5 Steps to Create the Life You Deserve
by Francine Huss. $16.95, 978-1-938314-66-7. With the help of
this guide, readers will learn to cultivate more creative thoughts,
realign their mindset, and gain a new perspective on life.

*This Way Up: Seven Tools for Unleashing Your Creative Self and
Transforming Your Life* by Patti Clark. $16.95, 978-1-63152-
028-0. A story of healing for women who yearn to lead a fuller
life, accompanied by a workbook designed to help readers work
through personal challenges, discover new inspiration, and har-
ness their creative power.

*Falling Together: How to Find Balance, Joy, and Meaningful
Change When Your Life Seems to be Falling Apart* by Donna
Cardillo. $16.95, 978-1-63152-077-8. A funny, big-hearted self-
help memoir that tackles divorce, caregiving, burnout, major illness, fears, and low self-esteem—and explores the renewal that
comes when we are able to meet these challenges with courage.

*The Clarity Effect: How Being More Present Can Transform
Your Work and Life* by Sarah Harvey Yao. $16.95, 978-1-63152-
958-0. A practical, strategy-filled guide for stressed professionals
looking for clarity, strength, and joy in their work and home lives.

*The Way of the Mysterial Woman: Upgrading How You Live,
Love, and Lead* by Suzanne Anderson, MA and Susan Cannon,
PhD. $24.95, 978-1-63152-081-5. A revolutionary yet practical
road map for upgrading your life, work, and relationships that
reveals how your choice to transform is part of an astonishing
future trend.